Eric Hosking's
WADERS

Eric Hosking's
WADERS

ERIC HOSKING
OBE, Hon. FRPS, FIIP
WITH
W.G. HALE
BSc, PhD, FIBiol
Professor of Animal Biology, Liverpool Polytechnic

FOREWORD BY
SIR PETER SCOTT

Pelham Books London

First published in Great Britain by
PELHAM BOOKS LTD
44 Bedford Square
London WC1B 3DU
1983

Photographs © Eric Hosking 1983
Text © W. G. Hale 1983

British Library Cataloguing in Publication Data
Hosking, Eric
   Eric Hosking's waders.
   1. Charadriiformes
   I. Title   II. Hale, W. G.
   598'.33   QL696.C4

ISBN 0 7207 1430 3

Typeset by Rowland Phototypesetting Ltd, Bury St
Edmunds, Suffolk

Printed and bound in Belgium by Brepols, Turnhout

AUTHOR'S NOTE

Since most waders are birds of Arctic and sub-Arctic
regions the seasons referred to in the text are those of
the northern hemisphere.

ENDPAPERS: Wrybills in flight

TITLE PAGE SPREAD: Blacksmith Plovers photographed
by a lakeside in Zimbabwe.

DEDICATION PAGE: Curlew

Contents

*This book is dedicated
to His Royal Highness
The Prince Philip,
Duke of Edinburgh,
President of the World Wildlife
Fund, who has done so much to
preserve our animal
inheritance.*

Foreword

by Sir Peter Scott

Waders have always held a particular fascination for me, although the ducks, geese and swans, which so often share the same marshes and estuaries, have been the subject of my life-long specialist studies. Some of the reasons for this delight in waders are that they look so elegant and graceful and that their calls are so evocative. Then there is the wonder of their still mysterious and amazingly long migrations. But also, for me and, I believe, for many other bird watchers, there is the challenge of a group of birds which are manifestly difficult to identify, and it is where the differences are subtle that photographs can be most helpful, because they record the distinctions of shape far more authoritatively than can any drawn illustrations in a field guide.

Eric Hosking has assembled in this book the finest collection of wader photographs I have ever seen, which reflects the mastery of his art by a man who has long been our leading bird photographer. As the only remaining original editor of the New Naturalist series, it was appropriate that Eric should turn to Professor Hale to write the text for this book, for it was he who wrote the book on waders in that famous series. He has worked hard and effectively for the conservation of wader habitat, and his part in saving the Ribble Marshes, subsequently designated as a National Nature Reserve, is well known. He also has extensive experience of scientific research on wading birds, and his passion for Redshanks is shown by the number of Eric's photographs of that species he has selected for this book.

Some years ago, Bill Hale brought Dianne Breeze to Slimbridge to show me some of her drawings, and it is nice to find that the only illustrations in this book that are not photographs are paintings by her of two species which were thought to be important. Neither the Ibis-bill nor the Seed Snipe is a typical wader but illustrations of them are few so that these certainly add considerable interest to the book.

Many of Eric's photographs catch the atmosphere of the wild places in which waders live and the book as a whole covers the full spectrum of wader biology. Particularly attractive are the photographs taken on

7

Hilbre Island in the Cheshire Dee, where the birds that feed on the mudflats of the estuary congregate at high tide. A number of bird photographers have set up their hides on Hilbre, but few, if any, have had such striking success as Eric. His work is eminently distinctive and probably no other single photographer could have brought together such a fine collection of wader pictures. From Antarctic Sheathbills to high Arctic Knots, Eric has followed his waders over most of the globe, and as their chronicler Bill Hale provides world-wide coverage of their natural history.

The book provides convincing evidence of the importance of wetland conservation at a time when these habitats are still being destroyed at an alarming rate all over the world.

My long-time friends have made a beautiful book and I am grateful to them, and to the publishers, for doing so, and for allowing me to be associated with it through this Foreword.

Peter Scott

Slimbridge
April 1982

Introduction

by W. G. Hale

Eric Hosking has pursued waders with his camera all over the world, and they have had a special attraction for him since he was introduced to the wintering flocks on the Cheshire Dee in 1946. So fascinated was he that since then he has visited the Dee every year, with only one exception. In his autobiography, he vividly describes his first experiences photographing wader flocks from a hide on Hilbre Island, and there is no doubt that his marvellous photographs have fired the enthusiasm for birds in many people. To be in a hide in the middle of a roosting flock of waders, or to be present just a few feet away from a bird settling on its eggs, are experiences which must be had first-hand to be fully appreciated. Yet somehow Eric Hosking manages to get some of this atmosphere into his photographs. For this reason, and the fact that they contained quite the best photographs of birds available, eight of his books were amongst the first bird books that I possessed. I have no doubts that his superb series of photographs of Greenshanks at the nest, and waders on Hilbre Island, were at least partially instrumental in my ornithological interests turning to this group of birds. His photographs have also inspired many other budding ornithologists and there are few who have not been stimulated by his work.

Whilst Eric has taken many wonderful photographs, for me his waders have always held a particular fascination. The famous wader pictures of the Greenshank removing an egg shell from the nest, the Stone Curlew staring hypnotically from her eggs, or the Knots asleep at high tide, are well known to almost everyone interested in birds. An Eric Hosking photograph somehow carries with it the stamp of the master; it is often immediately recognizable as his work. It was, then, with more than a little enthusiasm that I agreed to write the text for *Eric Hosking's Waders*. Looking through the photographs and choosing them for the book, made me even more aware that here was not only a wonderful collection of wader pictures, but a series illustrating the whole of the biology of the group. This was no mere assembly of portraits, excellent though they were; they represented a record of the lives of these birds which no other single collection could come near to matching.

Selecting the photographs for the book was no easy matter as there were so many to choose from. The most exciting moment for me was to discover that he had actually photographed one of my colour-marked Redshanks which had been ringed as a nestling on the Ribble Marshes. Obviously ringed birds spoil things for the photographer, but it certainly was a coincidence that one of my birds should pose for Eric!

The text of this book, designed to complement the photographs, describes something of the biology of wading birds and their lifestyles in different parts of the world. For the most part, waders are wetland birds and our wetlands are rapidly diminishing. Other wader habitat is being lost all over the world and active management and conservation measures must be undertaken to preserve wader populations. If this book stimulates an interest in waders in only a few people, it will have succeeded in at least one of its aims. The recognition that wading birds are a natural resource worth preserving takes us part of the way along the road to conserving one of our most attractive groups of birds, those which belong to the suborder Charadrii, the waders of Europe, the shorebirds of North America.

W. G. Hale
January 1982

Acknowledgements

by Eric Hosking

A wildlife photographer often finds himself indebted to numerous people and this is particularly so in my case because my work has taken me round the world. However, if everyone was mentioned, as perhaps they should be, the result would be just a list of names, so I have restricted my acknowledgements to those who have helped with this book.

Sir Peter Scott, internationally famous as a conservationist, as Vice President and Founder Chairman of the World Wildlife Fund and, of course, as a superb artist, has very kindly contributed the Foreword and I am extremely grateful to him.

How can I adequately express my thanks to Professor W. G. Hale for writing the text? He is the wader, or shorebird, expert of the world and his knowledge of these birds is limitless. Nobody can read this book without learning something new about this fascinating group.

My sincere thanks must go to Dr and Mrs Lewis MacAfee who since 1946 have held the annual Hilbre Party. This early autumn event has, let me confess, become more of a genial gathering than a photographic session. Many of the photographs were taken there.

To Herbert and Joan Axell I owe a lot. Herbert was for so many years the Warden of that famous Royal Society for the Protection of Birds' Reserve at Minsmere in Suffolk. The hides he erected for visitors proved ideal for the photographer.

On my numerous trips to East Africa, John Williams, Peter Davey and John Karmali have taken my wife and me to excellent sites for wader photography. John Williams helped us to secure pictures along the coast of Kenya, as well as inland, while Peter took us to Lake Jipe, where the numbers and variety of waders are remarkable. With John Karmali we enjoyed visits to Lakes Naivasha and Nakuru, renowned for their abundant water birds. Farther south in Africa, in Rhodesia, now Zimbabwe, Peter Steyn not only gave us splendid accommodation but also drove us to the best birdy places.

While in New Zealand, Geoff Moon and Ronald Lockley gave us VIP treatment when we spent a month travelling through the Islands. In Australia we met Graham Pizzey and Peter Slater, both authors of guides to the birds of that Continent, who showed us the sites where waders could be found.

During our visit to California, Dr and Mrs Ralph Buchsbaum gave us generous hospitality and introduced us to Dr Ron Branson and Alan Baldridge, two fine ornithologists who took us to the best spots for shorebirds.

Before he retired, Guy Mountfort organized some wonderful expeditions and invited me to go on them. Thus in the Coto Doñana in south Spain, in Bulgaria, Hungary, Jordan, Pakistan and Bangladesh, I photographed for the first time birds whose portraits appear in this book.

Without the help of Desmond Nethersole-Thompson, surely one of our finest field ornithologists, I could never have photographed the Greenshanks in the Scottish Highlands.

There are just a few black and white photographs I did not take and I am pleased to include some by the late Niall Rankin whose 6½" x 4¾" (16.5 x 12cm) glass negatives are now in my collection.

During my fifty-three years as a wildlife photographer I have managed to capture on film all the various wader families with the exception of the Ibis-bills. Until this year I had not portrayed any of the Seed Snipes, then Bill Hale discovered that there was one, the Least, at Birdland, Bourton-on-the-Water, that fine collection founded by the late Len Hill, and I was able to photograph it. In the meantime Bill had asked Dianne Breeze to paint the Ibis-bill and Seed Snipe and I am more than delighted to include her pictures in this book.

As usual I am greatly indebted to Barry Taylor and his staff at the Olympus Optical Company for their generous assistance – to my mind the OM-2n is the wildlife photographer's ideal camera.

Finally, and most importantly, without two members of my family this book would never have been produced. Dorothy, my wife, has suffered without complaint so many of the hardships that face a wildlife photographer. She has accompanied me to the Antarctic and the Arctic, to a great number of countries in between; throughout she has remained cheerful and ready to help. Our younger son, David, has supplied some of the photographs and has carried on our business on his own to leave me free to travel the world and work on this book. I cannot thank them both enough.

Eric Hosking
September 1982

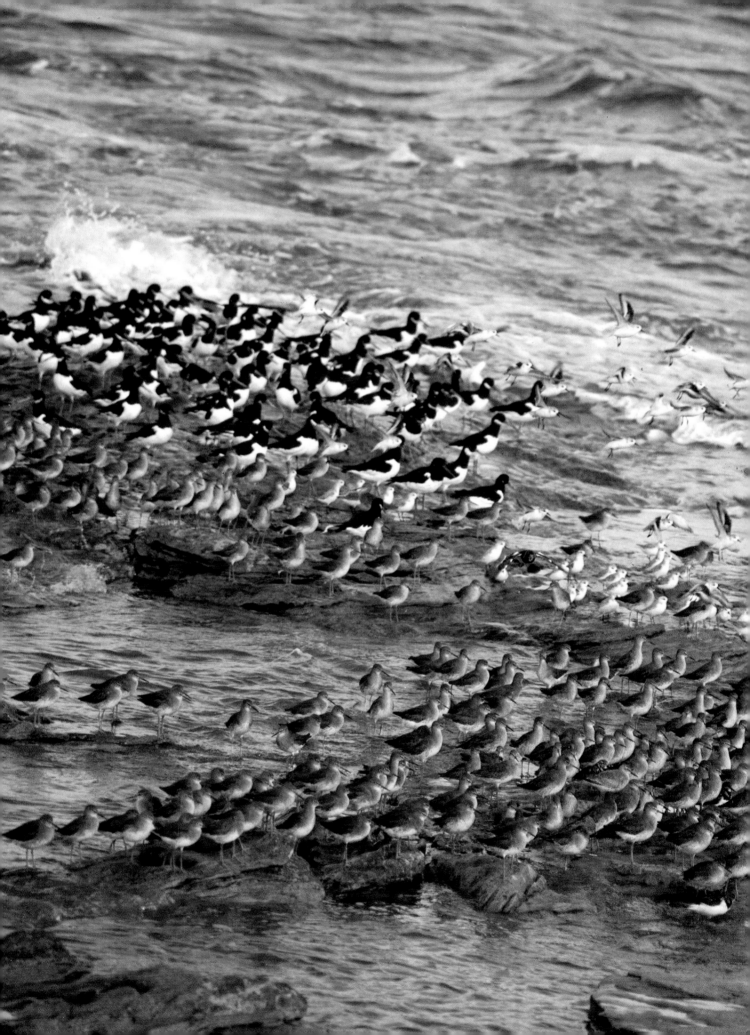

Waders' World

Scurrying along, stopping, pecking, running forward again, small, nondescript brown birds are a feature of the tide's edge almost anywhere in the world. Even an experienced birdwatcher may find identification difficult at times. The similarity between species and the variations in plumage at different times of the year, often cause confusion even between the commonest waders, but, even so, there are few groups of birds which hold such a fascination for the observer. Ranging in size from Stints which may be only 12 cm (4¾ ins) long and 21 g (7.4 oz) in weight, to the bigger Curlews (60 cm/24 ins and 1300 g/2 lb 14 oz) they are found along all our shores from the high Arctic to Australasia and there are even representatives in the Antarctic. Such is the success of the group that we can often see them literally in their thousands and, for example, flocks of Knots numbering up to one hundred thousand birds are not uncommon. These birds provide spectacular aerobatic exhibitions as they turn and catch the autumn sun, first flashing white, then black, rising into the air, twisting and falling to the glistening mudflats beneath, to roost. There can be few sights in the natural world more awe-inspiring.

For most of us, the place to see waders is on the shoreline as it is in this habitat that a great number of species spend the major part of the year. During the summer months many are to be found in the Arctic, nesting on the tundra and open grasslands of the north. At all times they are birds of wild places and their plaintive calls are the characteristic sounds of marsh and mudflat.

There are two major families of waders: the Plovers (Charadriidae) and the Sandpipers (Scolopacidae). These are placed together in the suborder Charadrii, in the order Charadriiformes, and contain most of the two hundred or so species in existence today. Whilst they are all collectively termed 'waders' or, in North America, 'shorebirds', the two main groups are not necessarily closely related. In fact, some authorities regard them as no more closely related than they are to the other major groups within the order Charadriiformes, which includes the Gulls and

13

the Auks. Generally speaking, Plovers are short billed, short legged and contrastingly coloured, whereas Sandpipers are long billed, long legged and for the most part dull in colour.

A minority of waders does not conveniently fall into either of the major categories, though relationships to one or other of these groups are established. These are placed in the remaining ten families of the suborder Charadrii:

Western Sandpipers – little brown, non-descript birds feeding at the edge of the tide.

Jacanidae	Jacanas (Lily-trotters)
Rostratulidae	Painted Snipes
Haematopodidae	Oystercatchers
Recurvirostridae	Avocets and Stilts
Burhinidae	Stone Curlews (Thick-knees)
Glareolidae	Coursers and Pratincoles
Dromadidae	Crab Plovers
Ibidorhynchidae	Ibis-bills
Thinocoridae	Seed Snipes
Chionididae	Sheathbills

The Jacanas and Painted Snipes are probably more closely related to the Plovers than to the Sandpipers, as are the Oystercatchers, Avocets, Stilts, Stone Curlews, Coursers and Pratincoles. The Sandpipers' close

RIGHT This Grey or Black-bellied Plover blends well into the background of the tundra, as do the eggs.

PAGE 12 Oystercatchers, Redshanks and Sanderlings on Hilbre Island.

14

Knots pack tightly both on the ground and in the air, and often perform complex and exciting manoeuvres over the mudflats.

relations are the Turnstones, Phalaropes, Snipes and Woodcocks (all placed in sub-families of the Scolopacidae), whilst small groups such as the Crab Plover, Ibis-bill and Seed Snipes are of uncertain affinities. However, they are all regarded as waders and they have a long evolutionary history going back as far as the Cretaceous period in the known fossil record. These ancient waders have been found in the fossil beds of New Jersey and Wyoming in the USA, and were birds of an era warmer than the present. There were no Arctic birds then as ice was absent from the earth's surface and the species that we now see have evolved in the intervening 70 million years. Clearly, waders have been around for a long time.

Despite their antiquity, the general body-form has not changed much since their oldest ancestors were alive. *Paleaotringa* looked very much like present-day Tringine Sandpipers, e.g. Redshanks and Yellowlegs, and *Ceramornis* had much the appearance of a Stilt. Both these birds lived between 65 and 70 million years ago and are thus more than four times older than the first-known passerine (singing) bird. The earliest Painted Snipe occurred in the Eocene, *c.*48 million years ago, and from the Montmartre deposits in France comes the first fossil placed in a modern genus – a Godwit (*Limosa gypsorum*). Godwits, then, must have lived for some 40 million years, probably twice as long as Oystercatchers and Stone Curlews, which appear as fossils in the Lower

15

Miocene. By the time Man appeared on earth most modern waders were in existence and thus have a history more than thirty times longer than our own species.

Today there are just over 8,500 species of living birds. James Fisher, the well-known ornithologist, estimated that under half a million species have existed in the 140 million years since *Archaeopteryx* lived, and it has been suggested that as many as 1½ million may not be an overestimate. Clearly a lot of species have died out and many of these must have been waders. Those which have survived have done so because their adaptations have enabled them to spread into every continent and to colonize many different habitats. Two small groups, the Jacanas and Painted Snipes, are tropical and sub-tropical representatives of the waders and occur in South America, Africa, India, Southeast Asia and Australia. The Jacanas have very much enlarged toes which enable them to spread their weight on the leaves of the aquatic vegetation over which they walk and on which they nest. The eggs are very shiny and water runs off the surface easily, which is of advantage as they are often submerged during incubation and when the bird leaves the fragile nest. In most species both sexes incubate but the Pheasant-tailed Jacana, an Asiatic species, is polyandrous – the female produces up to ten clutches which are incubated by different males. This is also the case in the Painted Snipes, which, like the Jacanas, lay a clutch of four

Plovers characteristically have both a short bill and short legs. The Killdeer Plover is typical of the group.

16

ABOVE Turnstones are circumpolar, breeding along the coasts of the Arctic ocean and south to Denmark.

The Spur-winged Plover is a typical Lapwing; many Lapwings possess a crest and wattles which play a part in courtship and aggressive behaviour.

eggs, in contrast to the clutch of two laid by the South American Painted Snipes and incubated by the female. Both Jacanas and Painted Snipes are associated with fresh water for most of their lives; Jacanas show some similarities to Coots and Gallinules in having a horny shield at the base of the bill and Painted Snipes show convergencies with Rails in their skulking habits and reluctance to fly. When they do so, like Rails, they trail their legs.

The more familiar Oystercatchers are noisy but attractive birds. There are possibly as many as ten species – five black and five black and white – but there is argument about the status of several of these and some taxonomists recognize only six species. All are very similar and, with the exception of the inland-breeding Asiatic population and some European birds, most are coastal throughout the year. With the chisel-like bill they break into shellfish such as cockles and mussels and knock limpets off rocks with a sharp blow. All this wears the bill and unlike other waders, Oystercatchers have a continuously growing bill. During the course of a year it has been estimated that growth of the 7-cm (2¾-in.) long bill may exceed 15 cm (6 ins). In other words, the normal length of bill is eroded twice a year.

In contrast to the massive beaks of the Oystercatcher, Avocets and Stilts have slender bills associated with feeding on small invertebrates. Stilts, as the name implies, have extremely long legs which enable them to wade deeply, but to feed in the shallows or on dry ground they have to bend them. At the nest the legs appear more than a little in the way and it is amusing to watch a Stilt settle on its eggs. In flight, the legs trail behind like a long tail. Whereas Stilts pick invertebrate food and seeds from the water surface and the shallows, the four species of Avocets take food with sweeping motions of the bill, usually in shallow water 5–10 cm (2–4 ins) deep, where they take animal food almost exclusively.

The Stone Curlews, or Thick-knees, look rather Plover-like but have exceptionally large eyes, associated with feeding at dusk and at night. They take mainly beetles and grasshoppers with their short, strong bills but they have been known to feed on molluscs, small reptiles and even small mammals. They are birds of open habitat and, in many parts of the world, semi-desert conditions. Their hunting technique is reminiscent of that of Herons: they will remain motionless for long periods and then walk slowly and deliberately, pausing again before darting the bill at the prey.

In contrast, the movements of the true Plovers are quick. Like the Stone Curlews they will 'freeze', but between the 'freezes' are fast runs. Often movement draws attention to them; when they are motionless they can be difficult to spot. Lapwings and Ringed Plovers tend to have disruptive plumage – bands of contrasting colours which break up the outline – whereas Golden Plovers have cryptic colouring which blends

OPPOSITE The African Jacana is also known as the Lily-trotter because of its habit of walking on floating vegetation.

BELOW The Stone Curlew has very large eyes which help in its search for food in twilight.

ABOVE Banded Stilts and Bar-tailed Godwits.

into the background because it is a similar colour and pattern. Lapwings differ markedly from other Plovers, particularly in the possession of rounded wings, and some have crests and face wattles. The shape of the wings is probably connected with their association with drier habitats, and the crest and wattles play a part in courtship and aggressive behaviour. Lapwings are among the most southerly breeding waders, with species throughout Africa and all the zoo-geographical regions* except the Nearctic (North America), though they are absent from the Arctic Circle. Within the Arctic Circle Golden Plovers and Ringed Plovers occur commonly. Whilst the latter occur in temperate regions all the year round, the former are common as passage migrants and in spring and early autumn their summer plumage provides a splash of colour on mudflats and grazed meadows.

Coursers are rather like Plovers with short wings and long legs adapted for running, and they are typically found in desert conditions. The closely related Pratincoles, known as Swallow Plovers because of their long wings and forked tail, are adapted to take insects on the wing, much in the manner of true Swallows. It is only when they alight and

OPPOSITE Sandpipers tend to have a long bill and long legs. This Greenshank, returning to the nest, shows these features well.

* Neotropical = Central and S. America; Nearctic = N. America and Greenland; Palaearctic = Eurasia and N. Africa; Ethiopian = Southern Africa and Madagascar; Oriental = India, Malaysia and parts of Indonesia; Australasian = Australia, New Zealand and New Guinea.

run forward that they appear in any way like Plovers. Often they will raise their wings above the back, a habit which is common in other waders and which reveals their likely relationships.

Whereas Plovers are generally colourful, particularly in summer, Sandpipers are for the most part, dull-coloured, though some species have reddish breeding plumage. Drab they may be, but in their range of adaptations, particularly of bill form, they are a most interesting group. They are birds of more northerly regions than the Plovers and they are highly migratory. The biggest representatives are the Curlews, with long legs and a long down-curved bill. Like the Shanks, they are adapted to feeding in deep vegetation. The smallest species, the Stints, nest in short vegetation on tundra. Sandpipers tend to form much bigger flocks than Plovers, and Knots often congregate in numbers exceeding 50,000 birds. During the last century the Eskimo Curlew was famous in North America for its migratory flights which contained thousands of birds. Wholesale slaughter (caused by extensive shooting) occurred, mainly during the spring passage, and probably contributed significantly to the near-demise of the species. Now only a few individuals remain. The closely related Little Curlew or Little Whimbrel, which nests in eastern Siberia, is not in immediate danger of extinction and lives in an interesting association with Golden Eagles. Where these eagles' eyries occur, small groups of Little Curlews nest and they seem to derive

ABOVE Phalaropes have an almost continuous distribution throughout the Arctic; the Red-necked (Northern) Phalarope, shown here at the nest, has a more southerly distribution than the Grey (Red) Phalarope.

ABOVE RIGHT Collared Pratincole at nest. Pratincoles are related to Plovers and because of their forked tail and long wings are known as Swallow Plovers.

PAGE 24 Black-tailed Godwit feeding. Godwits are known to have lived for at least 65 million years — more than thirty times as long as Man.

PAGE 25 An Oystercatcher approaches its nest. In its bill is a small beetle. The Oystercatcher is a cosmopolitan species and, surprisingly, seldom feeds on oysters.

benefit from this – possibly the eagles affect the numbers of other predators.

Different, but closely related, species of waders often occur in similar habitat types in North America and Eurasia. The European Curlew is replaced by the Long-billed Curlew in North America, the Bar-tailed[†] and Black-tailed Godwits of Eurasia are largely replaced by the Hudsonian and Marbled Godwit, and in the Shanks the New World species of Lesser and Greater Yellowlegs are represented by the Redshank, Greenshank and Spotted Redshank of the Old World. The latter three species show an interesting ecological separation across Eurasia, the Redshank occurring in the south of the range in temperate areas, the Greenshank in boreal areas and the Spotted Redshank extending into the tundra zone.

Several species have a circumpolar distribution. The Whimbrel, once known as the Hudsonian Curlew in North America, and species such as Dunlin, Red-necked and Grey Phalarope (Northern and Red Phalaropes of North America) have an almost continuous distribution throughout the Arctic; the Knot, Purple Sandpiper and Sanderling are also circumpolar in their breeding distribution but there are large areas where they do not breed.

The Ruddy Turnstone is found throughout the Arctic coastal regions but the Black Turnstone is confined to Alaska; however, both species

† Bar-tailed Godwits also breed in Alaska.

23

migrate south in autumn. These species are more truly shorebirds throughout the year than any other waders and in winter are found in the company of Purple Sandpipers on rocky shores where they find their food under stones and seaweed.

Phalaropes are birds of the water and the Grey Phalarope spends most of its life associated with the sea, near which it usually nests. The Red-necked and the Grey Phalarope are birds of the Arctic, but Wilson's Phalarope nests farther south in North America and winters in South America.

Woodcocks are the only group of waders to frequent woodland. They choose woods with damp floors which are not too acidic, for there earthworms flourish. Apart from the European and North American species, there are three Oriental Woodcocks. All have long beaks, relatively short legs and eyes set well back. Snipes are closely related to Woodcocks and are of similar body-form. Generally they are birds of temperate regions and the Common (Wilson's) Snipe is a cosmopolitan species breeding across Eurasia in eastern and southern Africa, North and South America. It also occurs in India where it is known as the Fantail Snipe. Of the thirteen species, possibly the most interesting is the Sub-Antarctic Snipe which nests in burrows excavated by other birds; it flies little and is mainly nocturnal. Dowitchers, at one time thought to be related to Godwits, are now considered nearer to Snipes, but unlike the latter they perform long migrations.

Like the Sub-Antarctic Snipe, Crab Plovers nest in burrows, each some 1½ m (5 ft) long, and the latter species excavates its own nest site. Like many hole-nesting birds, the Crab Plover lays a white egg which is comparatively large (as big as a Mallard's) for the size of bird. Lack of shell pigmentation and reduction in clutch size are typical of hole-nesting birds and in the case of the Crab Plover, the chick also lacks a pattern and is fed by the adults.

There are other aberrant groups of waders: Seed Snipes have evolved into seed eaters, and look like small Partridges; the Ibis-bill is similar to an Ibis, with a down-curved bill which it uses to probe under rounded stones in the shingly river beds of central Asia; and Sheathbills (two species) have colonized the Antarctic where their pure white plumage and association with the shoreline have given rise to the name of Kelp Pigeon.

Waders live in a changing world, much of which is being altered because of Man's activities. Drainage of wetlands threatens their wintering areas and the breeding grounds of some species such as Redshank. Recreational activities affect the nesting sites of some coastal Plovers but, for the most part, waders have so far benefited from changes brought about by Man. Felling of woodlands to make way for agricultural land has extended the habitat of several species of Plovers.

26

ABOVE Redshanks breed in a band across Eurasia north of latitude 70°N in Scandinavia but falling to 55°N in eastern Siberia. Roosting Redshanks are seen here with Knots and a single Grey Plover, still in summer plumage.

RIGHT Spotted Redshanks breed right across northern Eurasia up to 73°N in the Siberian Taimyr Peninsula.

Clearance of uplands has provided tundra-like habitat in many places, and woodland and upland management for game has assisted Woodcock, Golden Plover and Dunlin populations in Europe. Careful conservation strategies have maintained and even expanded populations of other threatened species, and whilst the ranges of some – e.g. Kentish (Snowy) Plovers – have contracted, others – e.g. Ruff, Black-tailed Godwit and Little Ringed Plover – have extended. The last mentioned has been aided by the provision of suitable nesting habitat as new gravel pits have been excavated, and common species such as the Eurasian Curlew have extended their range through changes in habitat preferences, moving on to tilled land in Germany. This was probably brought about when the bogs on which the Curlews nested were ploughed and the birds returned to breed on these areas. Elsewhere the Curlew has moved down to river valleys from the moors and Oystercatchers have moved inland to breed in river valleys. Whilst this is not directly attributable to human influences it is clear that Man has helped the spread of several species of wading bird. It is to be hoped that in the drainage of our wetlands we retain enough to ensure adequate areas for wintering waders. Conservation is a balance between the needs of Man and those of Nature. We must get the balance right.

ABOVE The Golden Plover, originally a tundra nester, has colonized uplands cleared of trees.

ABOVE LEFT The Little Ringed Plover – a species which has spread in western Europe and often nests in gravel pits.

OPPOSITE ABOVE The Crab Plover is a bird of the coasts of the Arabian Gulf and the Indian Ocean. It is the only wader to lay a white egg and it nests in burrows.

The Bar-tailed Godwit is a common wader on western European shores in winter.

28

Evolution

Today we think of many species of waders as being birds of cold climates, inhabiting the Arctic tundra during the short breeding season. Since the first waders were birds of warm habitats, the species which have become adapted to colder areas have clearly evolved later. The world remained warm until the mid-Miocene period (c.16 million years ago) but it took a further 14½ million years before the circumpolar belt of tundra was fully formed at the end of the Pliocene. At this time the climate of the world was similar to that of today and probably many wader species as we now know them had evolved. The last million years have seen the Arctic waders extend and contract their populations with the advancing and retreating glaciers of the great ice ages. In the interglacial periods the populations of these waders withdrew to refuges in northern Greenland, Alaska and eastern Siberia. As the ice pushed south, the tundra increased its area as it did so and this provided more habitat suitable for Arctic birds. Thus it can be assumed that the biggest populations probably existed at the time of the southern-most extension of the ice. The last ice age was at its height between 17,000 and 20,000 years ago and developed over a period of 80,000 years from the mid-interglacial. At this time the biggest tundra refuge was in northern Greenland and it is likely that species such as Knot, Turnstone, Dunlin, Ringed and Golden Plovers were then restricted to this area. As the ice sheet extended so these populations spread into North America and northern Europe, increasing in numbers and occupying the new tundra. Different species spread out from the other refuges: from eastern Siberia – Long-billed Dowitchers, Wandering Tattler, Great Knot, Red-necked and Long-toed Stints; and from Alaska – Short-billed Dowitchers, Hudsonian Godwit and White-rumped Sandpiper. Some of these species were limited to relatively small geographical areas, whereas others, e.g. Dunlin, spread throughout the available habitat. Meanwhile to the south, temperate species extended even farther south.

It is probably true to state that all species of waders have arisen through being geographically isolated from other similar populations

31

for long periods of time. Many arose through isolation during the ice ages while others, less fortunate, died out as a result of the changing climates of their refuges. Often it is easy to see which species are most closely related. For example, the Golden Plover of Europe is clearly related to the Lesser Golden Plover of Asia and North America and slightly more distantly related to the Grey or Black-bellied Plover which occupies a similar range to the latter species. In Europe the Spotted Redshank, Redshank and Greenshank are close relatives of and replaced in North America by the Lesser and Greater Yellowlegs. Almost certainly all these species have evolved in isolation from each other and have come together again in parts of their ranges at a later stage.

Sometimes populations are separated for periods too short for development to full species, and in other cases the range is so great that effectively those at the extremities are isolated. Here it is not unusual to find differences in colour, size, behaviour or physiology of a magnitude which has resulted in the different forms being given sub-specific, or trivial, names. Thus, in the case of the Dunlins of north-east Greenland, which are smaller and redder than those of northern Scandinavia, the former are referred to as *Calidris alpina arctica*, the latter as *C. a. alpina*. It does not always follow that because a species has an extensive range, sub-species will occur. In the Lapwing, for example, there is no geographical variation throughout the range, which extends across

32

ABOVE Turnstones nest high in the Arctic and like Knots were probably limited to a refuge in Greenland in warmer times.

ABOVE LEFT The Black Turnstone has a much more restricted range than the more common (Ruddy) Turnstone, and may well have occupied an Alaskan refuge in the last interglacial period.

OPPOSITE The Long-billed Dowitcher almost certainly originated in an eastern Siberian refuge.

PAGE 30 The Black Stilt of New Zealand is another colour form of the Black-winged Stilt.

Eurasia. However, in forms where different colour variants occur, they tend to do so in the same places so that Greenland, northern Scandinavia and eastern Siberia each have their own colour forms (races) of several species of wader. It may well be that each of these areas was associated with its own particular glacial refuge and in each of these refuges were isolated populations of several different species. North America has a number of species replacing Eurasian ones, but in the case of the Dunlin three colour forms are found there, one of which spreads across the Bering Straits to Asia.

One of the most interesting aspects of geographical variation in waders concerns the phenomenon of 'northern' and 'southern' populations. Here species of sub-Arctic breeding waders – the 'northern' birds – have variants far to the south of the normal range. Dunlins and Golden Plovers breeding in the region of the British Isles and the Baltic do not have such a rich summer plumage as those breeding farther north, and particularly in the Golden Plover many individuals of the 'southern' birds breed in almost full winter plumage. A similar situation arises in the Redshank, Black-tailed Godwit and Ringed Plover; though these are not normally referred to as 'southern' forms, the lack of a full breeding plumage is the same. There could be several reasons for this. It is just possible that a breeding plumage is a disadvantage to birds which nest south of their normal range as they may not be so well camouflaged

Like most other Lapwings the Crowned Lapwing is a bird of warm climates.

BELOW Sanderlings, cold climate waders which nest in the high Arctic.

on southern grasslands as opposed to northern tundra. Alternatively the southern populations may have been derived from birds which for some physiological reason did not undergo a normal moult nor migrate north in the spring, or whose diet in the southern breeding area or in coastal regions may possibly have affected the moult. Again, energy normally required for moulting could have been utilized in earlier breeding, or in the case of the Dunlin the plumage might vary in an attempt to mimic that of the Golden Plover, with which it associates during the breeding season, being known as the Plover's Page in the British Isles and the Plover's Slave in Scandinavia.

A more likely explanation is that populations of the same species which had been separated for a long period of time (thousands of years) in Greenland, Iceland and Scandinavia, came together in the region of the British Isles and the southern Baltic and produced vigorous hybrids. Climatic deterioration in these areas was probably the cause and it led to a more southerly breeding distribution of the species concerned. It appears that these possible hybrids possessed characteristics which enabled them to remain much farther north in winter than their parent populations. The spring moult may well have been affected as these birds have only a partial breeding plumage and most individuals fail to lose many of their winter feathers in spring.

Are these birds without a summer plumage at a disadvantage? It would seem not: certainly the Redshank hybrids without breeding dress are able to obtain mates and breed just as successfully as those non-hybrids with it. Possible reasons for this success are that they breed earlier and raise more chicks. It is also interesting to note that large forms of the Redshank and Ringed Plover have spread into southern Norway and Sweden during this century and replaced the smaller, later-breeding non-hybrid birds which originally occupied this area. The latter may now be extinct in Scandinavia, but there are several skins in museum collections to show that they existed there until recently.

Where an animal assumes a breeding dress during the nesting season and it is clearly of use only at this time, then the selection for this dress must take place on the breeding grounds. It is reasonable to assume that under normal circumstances those animals possessing such characteristics are at an advantage to those lacking them, and these features will therefore be selected for. Characters possessed only at certain times of the year are clearly selected for then, but others are present throughout life, e.g. bill length, tarsus (leg) length, overall size, and it is more difficult to decide where these are selected for and for what purpose.

It has been suggested that selection for size in Redshanks and Ringed Plovers took place in winter since it was only at this time that different western European breeding populations were arranged with the smallest in the south and the largest in the north. This would fit in with the

This Spanish-breeding Redshank has a full breeding plumage.

BELOW It is likely that Knots were confined to Greenland during the last interglacial period.

ecological principle known as Bergmann's Rule which states that warm-blooded animals of any one species tend to be largest in the north (colder part) of the range. This is associated with heat loss through the body surface, and as larger animals have a smaller surface area to volume ratio they are therefore better suited to cold climates. When winter populations from throughout the range were examined in detail it was found that large and small birds, from different populations, occurred together in winter. It was not only small birds which wintered in the south of the range and large ones in the north. In the breeding season, size variation in any one geographical area was found to be small and it therefore seems likely that selection for this characteristic takes place on the nesting grounds. This is of particular interest in relation to bill size as it is often assumed that longer bills are specifically adapted to feeding in mud; during the breeding season, except in a few instances, this is seldom the case, so that we must look for other selective forces for producing long bills whose secondary function is probing in mud. Most long-billed waders are capable of opening the tip of the bill by bending the mandible (rhynchokinesis) and this clearly enables the bird to handle small objects more delicately than the hinge at the joint of the mandibles would allow. In Snipes this facility is certainly used in probing but in birds such as Godwits it is probably of great value in picking berries from the ground in vegetation, and it may well be that

long bills of some Sandpipers have evolved for just this purpose.

The fact that the smallest Redshanks nest farthest north, in northern Scandinavia, whilst the largest birds nest only slightly farther south, in Iceland, can be accounted for by the fact that the Scandinavian birds breed some four weeks later than the Icelandic birds and are thus subjected to higher temperatures on their arrival at the breeding grounds. This is interesting because here are two very different populations of birds of the same species which have evolved along very different lines. One is of large cinnamon birds which breed early and the other is of small dark-brown birds which breed late. Clearly these populations had evolved separately over a long period of time, but have not evolved to the species level.

If a character which an animal possesses is to be selected for, then those individuals which possess it must produce more young which survive to breed than their competitors. This is brought about either by breeding more often (or more successfully) where the adult mortality rates are similar, or, by surviving longer, which effectively is the same. As a survival strategy, then, breeding early, being larger and migrating only short distances, appears to be more successful than being small, breeding late and migrating long distances.

Whilst this selective mortality is important in determining the characteristics of a population, the mortality which regulates the numbers of birds may be of a different nature. Most variations in numbers fluctuate about a mean figure, and this is thought to be brought about by density-dependent factors. These act on a population more when it is high and less when it is low, and factors can be associated with either the birth rate (rarely) or the mortality rate (usually). With large populations the death rate is great or the birth rate low, and the reverse applies when the numbers are small. Whilst density-dependent loss of life may be selective, it is not necessarily so. Again much mortality may take place on the breeding grounds, but here it is likely that this affects the numbers of chicks reared. An example of how it might work is provided by the Redshank. Here, chicks are led to wet areas to feed as soon as they are hatched. In a relatively dry season such wet areas may be few so that not all the families can be accommodated. If the number of wet areas is limited more young will die through not finding suitable feeding areas if the population is high. The numbers dying depend on the density – the greater this is, the more individuals die. Little is known about how wader numbers are regulated and it is possible that mechanisms other than density-dependent factors play a part.

In any species of animal or plant there is considerable genetic variation which enables the organisms concerned to adapt quickly to change. Within, say, a population of mosquitoes are a few which are

ABOVE Waders have a flexible upper mandible which enables them to open the bill tip without opening the base of the bill. This can be clearly seen in the Dunlin above.

The Lapwing has an extensive range right across Eurasia where it shows no geographical variation. Possibly this is due to members of the species being less attached to their places of birth than are many other waders.

ABOVE The New Zealand Black Oyster-catcher is regarded as a melanic form of the common Oystercatcher, *Haematopus ostralegus*.

ABOVE RIGHT The American Black Oyster-catcher is considered to be a good species *Haematopus bachmani*.

OPPOSITE The Golden Plover varies from retaining almost all its winter plumage during the breeding season to having a completely black breast.

PAGES 44–5 The Black-necked Stilt is merely a colour variant of the Black-winged Stilt, *Himantopus himantopus*. Here they are seen with two Greater Yellowlegs.

resistant to insecticides such as DDT. When this is used only the resistant forms survive, and the new population arising from these individuals is itself DDT resistant. Exactly the same situation occurs in all animals. In waders, for example, the majority of any one population has evolved the type of breeding strategy to produce the largest numbers of survivors. We have briefly touched on timing of breeding but some species have evolved other mechanisms. In the Sanderling, Canadian birds produce two clutches in quick succession, and, whilst one is incubated by the female, the other is attended by the male. In contrast, in Greenland the incubation of one clutch is shared. It seems likely that more chicks are hatched per pair in Canada than in Green-land, but each strategy is the best for that particular area. There are always a few birds in any population which differ genetically from the others and these are sometimes equipped to deal with changes which might occur. A close look at a flock of Turnstones in summer plumage shows that no two birds have exactly the same head pattern and, in any group of waders, close examination reveals differences between indi-viduals. It is on these genetic differences that evolution works.

All wader characters – banding patterns, wing bars, call notes, behavioural traits – have become part of the genetic make-up because they are of use at some stage of the life history. Every character plays a part, at some time, in the survival of a species. For millions of years,

43

ABOVE The Wrybill shows an interesting adaptation of the beak, from whence it gets its name. The curve facilitates the removal of invertebrates from under stones.

LEFT Ruff in moult; a bird acquiring its summer plumage.

Curlew with chicks. The young, led by the adults, often walk long distances immediately after hatching when the parents take them to suitable feeding areas. In dry seasons young birds may have great difficulty in finding food.

wading birds have contended with environmental changes, and while many species have survived, others have died out. Now the habitat is changing not so much because of natural factors, but because of human influences. Different pressures are being brought to bear on the waders, particularly those which winter in temperate areas where there are large human populations. The effects of pollution are most dramatically seen in oiled seabirds, or in the reduction in numbers of birds of prey through the use of organo-chlorine seed-dressings and insecticides. Such problems are well publicised, but less well known are the effects of organic lead which finds its way into estuarine birds and is lethal in very small doses. Waders are clearly vulnerable.

There can be no doubt that, like many other animals, waders will be increasingly subjected to human influences in their environment. But there is reason for optimism. We have seen that many species have actually increased as a result of Man's influence and others are holding their own; the mere recognition that there is a threat to our wading birds is a significant step towards proper conservation measures. The critical factor is to retain sufficient of their natural environment – both breeding and wintering grounds. This will ensure that they can continue to combat natural changes in the same way as they have done for the past 70 million years.

47

Feeding and Foods

Whenever the topic of feeding in wading birds is raised, most birdwatchers' thoughts turn to the shore and to waders picking and probing for tiny morsels of food. Whilst it is easy to distinguish, say, a cockle being manipulated by an Oystercatcher, most food items are small and difficult to identify through binoculars or a telescope. The same problem is experienced when watching waders feeding inland in winter. It is probably because of this that feeding ecology appears to be less interesting than other aspects of wader biology, but like many other things the more you know about it, the more fascinating it becomes.

Stepping lightly across the mud, picking up something here, probing a little there, a feeding flock tends to move in the same general direction, the birds much more spaced out than when they are resting at the roost. In the breeding season most waders have moved from the shore to inland nesting areas, and here, clearly, they are not foraging for the same food. Marine invertebrates which inhabit the mudflats are replaced by adult insects and larvae, seeds, berries, earthworms, providing a summer diet which is markedly different from that in winter.

Depending upon what information is required about feeding, different techniques must be used to obtain it. Prey species can be identified from the gut contents of dead birds, from the disgorged meals of live birds (by using emetics), or from the careful examination of pellets, which many species of waders produce. However, if it is required to know how much food is taken in, then detailed information on the variations in the rate of intake due to differences in the stages of the tide cycle, the lengths of the day and night, the annual cycle and the weather conditions, must be obtained. Often feeding studies combine observation with examination of gut contents, and during recent years much emphasis has been placed on the study of estuarine feeding of waders, during the collection of evidence to combat reclamation of inter-tidal areas. Much of this work has been done by professional biologists, but there is one line of enquiry that anyone can follow: pellet examination.

Just like owls and raptors, many waders produce pellets of indigestible

ABOVE Red-necked Stints. Waders feeding in flocks always face the wind, turning occasionally from side to side.

OPPOSITE, ABOVE LEFT Plovers tend to pick food items from the surface or near to it, as this Ringed Plover is doing.

OPPOSITE, ABOVE RIGHT Common Snipe often use the whole length of the bill in probing or searching, as here, below water.

LEFT Dunlins and Ringed Plovers at high tide. Pellets can often be found amongst the droppings on roosting sites.

PAGE 48 Golden Plovers will also take berries in addition to insects whilst on the breeding areas.

material, at regular intervals. Some species, such as Curlews and Shanks, produce firm pellets, but Oystercatchers and Knots often regurgitate wet masses which immediately blend with the mud and are difficult to collect. However, when these species roost on closely cropped saltmarsh vegetation, distinct pellets can be found. Curlew roosts are excellent sites to get your 'eye in'. Their pellets are 2–3 cm (¾–1¼ ins) long and vary from being almost spherical to ovoid. They may contain stones, pieces of gravel and sometimes the cast, dried membrane of the gizzard lining which is shed at intervals. Finding traces of food in Curlew pellets can be difficult since most of the invertebrate food is digested, but frequently grass seeds, berries and the hard parts of crabs and other crustaceans can be seen. Pellets may contain pieces of mollusc shells which have been derived from a food item or have been taken in with gravel, which is purposely collected to help digestion. Pellets of Shanks are smaller and these species tend to take in tiny mineral particles, usually sand, when feeding on the shore. Whole shells of small marine snails and parts of shrimp-like organisms can easily be distinguished, and examination through a lens of a low-powered microscope may reveal the presence of jaws from marine worms.

Perhaps wader pellets are not quite as exciting as those from birds of prey but they do provide useful information on what waders eat. The shore roost is the easiest place to find them, but inland roosts at the

51

beginning of the breeding season, and later, near the nest, are sites to search.

If observation of the feeding birds is combined with pellet examination then identification of prey items becomes a little easier. On the shore small items picked up are almost certainly marine snails, such as *Hydrobia*, or small crustaceans, such as the shrimp – *Corophium*. Worms are also taken; in Godwits and Curlews these may be large lugworms (e.g. *Arenicola*) or smaller polychaet worms such as *Nereis*. The shoreline diet may also include a range of larger molluscs: cockles (*Cerastoderma*), mussels (*Mytilus*), limpets (*Patella*) and clams (e.g. *Mya*), smaller venus shells and other bivalves such as *Macoma*. Away from the shore, earthworms and the larvae of many insects, particularly leatherjackets (the larvae of crane flies), are commonly taken, and adult flies (*Diptera*) and beetles (*Coleoptera*) are important parts of the diet of many breeding waders. Berries are probably more significant in the summer diet than is generally appreciated. The small amount of research that has been done on feeding during the nesting season has shown berries to be present in the gut systems of Godwits, Curlews and Golden Plovers, at both the beginning and the end of the breeding season. It appears that the previous year's berries are of particular value to birds arriving in the Arctic when few insects have emerged. Again, in more temperate areas, Woodcocks are well known to feed extensively

ABOVE Grey or Black-bellied Plovers feed almost exclusively on marine invertebrates on the mudflats.

ABOVE LEFT The Whimbrel uses its long bill for taking berries during the breeding season.

Lapwings often feed in flooded fields.

on blackberries, and vegetable material probably plays a more important part in the diet of wading birds than is revealed by estuarine studies.

More is known about the feeding of waders on the shore than in any other habitat, and since many species spend the majority of their time there, clearly there is an adequate food supply. The invertebrate food species on which the waders prey are not distributed evenly over the mudflats, and like soil animals are apt to be highly aggregated. High sand banks which tend to dry out at the surface at low tide, do not provide suitable habitat for the invertebrates. These tiny creatures are usually found in wetter, lower areas, where the detritus on which they feed accumulates. This is washed down the rivers or off the saltmarsh, and some is brought in with the tide; it is the base of the food web on the estuary and supports vast numbers of animals on which the waders prey. Animals such as *Hydrobia* and *Corophium* are the commonest and may be present in tens of thousands to a square metre (yard). The former is often found at the surface when it is wet, and the latter occurs in burrows and has to be searched out. Small bivalve molluscs, e.g. *Macoma*, may be found in thousands to the square metre (yard) as can the errant worms, whereas in a similar-sized area the larger molluscs and lugworms are found in hundreds. Many, but not all, invertebrates present clues to their presence: worms produce casts and cavities in the mud, molluscs indicate their whereabouts by depressions and frequently the small burrows in which *Corophium* lives can be seen.

Beneath the mud there is plenty to eat – finding it is often another matter altogether. Different species have different techniques. In daylight, Oystercatchers in search of cockles probe the mud, apparently following surface clues; in the dark, however, they walk forward with an angled bill, moving the tip up and down in a 'sewing' motion until a cockle is located. Once it is found the bill is inserted and it is removed from the mud by sideways movements of the head. Then it is opened by a series of sharp blows aimed primarily at the adductor muscle which keeps the two valves of the shell closed. Mussels are opened in a similar fashion.

The smaller waders, 'peeps', often feed with a similar 'sewing' manner to that of the Oystercatcher and areas of mud with lace-like patterns show where they have been feeding. During this action, the bill is momentarily removed from the mud and stuck back in only a bill-width farther on, as the bird moves forward.

Waders collect a lot of their food from the surface, particularly *Hydrobia*, and even the casual observer will see that deep probing is the exception rather than the rule. It is perhaps surprising that long bills are always associated with probing, though, of course, many waders do engage in this activity. Godwits will remove lugworms from deep in their burrows; Snipes will probe deeply, too. Curlews will take lug-

55

ABOVE Wood Sandpipers are easily distinguishable from their near relatives because of their bolder markings and slimmer head and neck.

LEFT Some waders will defend feeding territories; a Spotted Redshank disputes a feeding site with a neighbour.

OPPOSITE Marsh Sandpipers often wade deeply in search of food.

BELOW Dunlins often feed throughout the period of high water.

The Curlew Sandpiper will often wade up to its belly whilst feeding.

worms but more frequently will be seen on the tide-line picking up small crabs. Several species feed actually in the water and take small fish in addition to invertebrates. Some are very specialist feeders.

Phalaropes often spin on their own axes when swimming, in order to disturb food from the bottom, and, like Stilts, will also pick it delicately from the surface. Avocets 'sweep' for very small items and on occasions other waders will exhibit a similar feeding motion, e.g. Greenshank. Pratincoles take insects on the wing and Stone Curlews will stalk their prey like Herons. Turnstones search for food items below pebbles, which they often move, and the aberrant Sheathbills scavenge and take other birds' eggs. For the most part, however, waders are pickers and probers. Plovers are not able to probe deeply because they have relatively short bills, so take food from only the top 2–3 cm (¾–1¼ ins). On the shore, in winter, many invertebrates are to be found at a greater depth than in summer – they migrate vertically – so a smaller proportion of their population is available to feeding birds. Knots, which often feed extensively on *Macoma*, are able to reach fewer than half the shellfish present in the mud in winter and this applies to many other species of waders and their prey. So, while food is there for the taking, it is not necessarily accessible. However, because a large part of the potential food supply is out of reach, it does not mean that birds are hard-pressed to find enough food.

ABOVE Surf Birds feed in amongst sea-weed, a habit shared with Turnstones and Purple Sandpipers.

RIGHT The Pectoral Sandpiper has a special fat reserve on which it can sustain itself should the breeding grounds be snow covered when it returns in spring.

A Green Sandpiper searches for invertebrate food.

OPPOSITE BELOW The Common Sandpiper searches the shallows at a lake edge for its food.

BELOW Like many other species of wader, Black-tailed Godwits will wade belly deep during feeding; in summer, insects and berries form a major part of their food.

It does not take wading birds very long to find the best food sources, and when they do so they tend to congregate in these areas. Even where food is plentiful birds will move to other areas if they can obtain food more easily elsewhere. A great deal of research has been carried out to determine what is known as the 'carrying capacity' of feeding areas; this is the maximum number of birds that an area can support. Because our intertidal areas are subject to so many environmental pressures it is important to know if the present wintering wader populations can be supported on smaller areas, but so far the results are inconclusive. It does appear that under normal circumstances, wading birds generally do not find difficulty in obtaining enough to eat except when food is inaccessible, for example during periods of hard frost.

If we think of the invertebrate food supply available in terms of an annual crop, only some 10 per cent of this is taken by waders. Some invertebrates are eaten in greater quantities than others, but 90 per cent of what is produced is not touched by waders. In some cases they are in competition with other animals, e.g. flat-fish and wildfowl, but on the whole they seem to take a smaller proportion of the available food than consumers in other habitats. Where there is a size range of a prey species available, waders take the bigger individuals.

It might be argued that if food is so easily come by some habits of waders need not have been evolved. Why, for example, do Dunlins feed throughout the normal roosting time, and why do many waders feed at night? Some species have to feed continuously in order to obtain enough to eat, particularly at times of the year when invertebrates are small (i.e. young). Others, such as Oystercatchers, obtain their daily food requirement quite quickly and so are able to spend much more time roosting. Oystercatchers often feed at night and it is very likely that feeding at low tide at this time is more profitable than it would be at mid-tide during the day.

It is only when life becomes difficult that these behavioural traits become important. For a character or a habit to be selected for, from an evolutionary point of view it need only be of value occasionally, and this is almost certainly the case in these instances.

It is now recognized that night feeding in waders is widespread. On the shore it occurs at all phases of the moon but inland it is particularly associated with the period of the full moon. Lapwings and Curlews will feed at night and sleep during the day at this time. No obvious explanation for this behaviour is available but it does seem that feeding during the full moon must be particularly profitable since some birds will make extensive journeys (15 miles in the case of Curlews) to feed on the shore. It may well be that food organisms are more active at this time and it is well known that some invertebrates exhibit a lunar periodicity in their behaviour. However, until more is discovered about

61

this subject, it will remain a source of intrigue.

Once waders arrive on their wintering areas, most individuals begin to put on weight. This is not surprising as they will have used up fat during the course of their migration and depositing more fat is an insurance against cold weather. Weight increases in most species up to the end of December, and in temperate areas more fat is deposited than farther south. From the beginning of January most species lose weight until just before the northerly migration when a rapid increase takes place. In this Oystercatchers are exceptional: they continue their weight increase throughout the winter. Weight changes appear to be controlled by an internal mechanism and are not directly influenced by the food supply. However, the very fact that weight increase is possible indicates that the supply is at least sufficient. In spring the rapid pre-migratory increase in weight is produced against a background of the smallest number of individuals in the invertebrate populations, just prior to their breeding. However, these individuals are at their maximum size and after the end of the winter have moved upwards in the mud, nearer to the surface, so are more readily available to the waders. Waders are literally very fat before they begin the northward movement.

Back on the breeding areas the food situation is often not so good. High Arctic breeders may arrive before the melt, when only small areas are clear of snow, and they may have to exist for a short time on their

OPPOSITE ABOVE The Red-necked Phalarope spins on the water surface to disturb food items from the bottom of a pool.

OPPOSITE BELOW An Avocet sweeps the water with its upturned bill to collect invertebrates in the surface layer.

BELOW The Stone Curlew stalks its prey in the manner of a Heron.

64

ABOVE A Water Dikkop displays as a Monitor enters its feeding area.

A Snowy Sheathbill feeding on a Penguin egg in a rookery of Chinstrap Penguins.

reserves. The Pectoral Sandpiper is particularly interesting in this respect in that it possesses a large, fat body which appears to be specifically evolved for this purpose. On temperate breeding areas there is little difficulty in finding food, though several species, e.g. Golden Plover, tend to eat away from the breeding area, thus to some extent preserving the potential food supply for later in the season.

There is scant information on feeding during the breeding season. What little exists suggests that waders experience more difficulty in obtaining food at this time of the year than at others. At the end of the breeding season one adult may leave the chicks to be tended by the other parent, and move south before the chicks fly. This could well be a mechanism to ensure sufficient food for the remaining birds.

We have seen what sort of food waders take, how and when they get it and from where, but how much of it do they require? If we are prepared to accept a Redshank as an 'average' wader, then this takes in some 50 g (roughly 2 oz) of food per day. Over a year it would take in over 100 times its own weight, that is, about 20 kg (44 lbs). An Oystercatcher may consume 150 times its own weight, up to 83 kg (182 lbs) in a year. Put in different terms this may be up to 280 cockles per Oystercatcher during one daylight tide, or up to 56 million cockles per daylight tide for the British wintering population! There can be no doubt that our wader populations need a lot of food. At the present time there is plenty there for them. Apart from ensuring that enough habitat is maintained, both in winter and during the breeding season, it is essential that wader habitats are subjected to the minimum amount of pollution. Both the marine invertebrate population of the wintering areas and the insect populations of the breeding grounds are particularly susceptible to human interference and it is just as important to conserve the food supplies as it is to conserve the habitat. Often poisonous substances find their way into animals through their food, as did the organo-chlorine compounds which badly affected our birds of prey. It is, therefore, very important to prevent food supplies being contaminated. So far, our waders have escaped relatively unscathed; we must keep it this way.

Breeding Behaviour

In temperate regions the onset of the breeding season is less noticeable than it is in the Arctic. In high latitudes the thaw of the snows normally coincides with the coming of the migrant waders, and a late melt delays their arrival. For Arctic waders the breeding season is a relatively short period of high activity whereas in warmer regions, it begins slowly and is a more drawn out affair.

Most temperate breeding waders arrive at their nesting areas five or six weeks before the first eggs are laid. In Europe, Oystercatchers tend to be back on their breeding grounds in February, and later in the month, Lapwings which have wintered on the coastal plains move to higher land. March sees Curlews and Redshanks moving inland. Long-distance migrants, such as Common Sandpipers and Greenshanks, tend to arrive later, but still there is a significant time lapse before the first eggs appear. This is not so in the Arctic. There breeding activities begin immediately the birds reach their destination and often birds arrive paired so that many aspects of courtship may be dispensed with.

In some species there is a tendency for one sex to arrive first on the breeding grounds: in Phalaropes, this is usually the female, whereas in several other cases, e.g. Dunlin, it is the male. In the Arctic, individuals of any one species are apt to arrive within a relatively short period of five to ten days, so often the sexes do travel together, but in temperate areas the drift back to the breeding areas may be spread over five or six weeks. Generally it is the older, more experienced birds that return first. These birds often retain their mate from the previous year so preliminary courtship is minimized. Younger birds tend to arrive later and those about to breed for the first time are usually the last to start nesting activities – they have to find a mate, and, in some cases, establish a territory. With experience comes earlier and more successful breeding.

Many waders are remarkably attached to the site of the previous year's nest and males will return to defend almost exactly the same piece of the breeding area. Territorialism is, perhaps, more evident in Plovers than in Sandpipers, and is an activity which occupies quite some time at

67

the beginning of the breeding season. In Lapwings rival males fly parallel to their boundaries, tilting at each other in flight; Ringed Plovers will display to each other on the ground at territory limits. In fact, several species of Plovers will react with aggression to their own images in mirrors.

Some species, e.g. Redshank, show no signs of territoriality in some parts of their range, being almost semi-colonial in places, with nests only a few metres apart. Where birds are territorial, nests are evenly spaced though in different parts of the range nest density varies.

As the season progresses, territory defence is indulged in less and less, and by the time the eggs hatch it is non-existent in most species. It seems, therefore, that the main point of territoriality is in limiting the nest density, and, in this way, limiting the breeding population. At least in some species, e.g. Dunlin, it appears to maintain a non-breeding population from which birds move in to the main breeding area when vacancies arise, through, say, predation. How non-territorial species such as Redshanks limit breeding density, if at all, is not known. The area appears to have little function in providing a food supply for the occupants at any time; early in the season the pair tends to feed elsewhere and when the young are hatched, boundaries no longer exist.

Male waders will defend a territory before they are paired, and in some cases, e.g. Curlew Sandpiper, will chase away species other than

Curlews moving inland to the breeding grounds.

PAGE 66 Black-winged Stilts indulge in courtship display.

68

ABOVE Many waders use wing lifting simply to rearrange the primary feathers, as in the Dunlin shown here.

ABOVE RIGHT The courtship display of the Redshank culminates in wing raising and wing quivering by the male bird.

their own. Ownership is often advertised by means of a display flight. However, such behaviour often has a different function and in Shanks and Curlews is used to attract a mate. In both these species, this flight is undulating, the rise being brought about by rapid beating of the wings and the fall by a glide, in the Shanks on decurved wings, in Curlews on raised wings. Usually a special 'song' is performed, with the aim of attracting a potential mate into the air. Some display flights are quite elaborate, and that of Snipes and Little Curlews includes 'drumming' in a dive. This sound is caused by the passage of air over the outer tail feathers and the undulating quality of the note by the wing beats. Where a display flight has a territorial function, in addition there may well be a quite distinct aerial display associated with pairing. This is the case in male Oystercatchers, whose 'butterfly flight' (so-called because of the slow rate of wing beat) appears to be aggressive and territorial in nature, whereas their 'whirring flight' (which features rapid wing beats) has a role in pair formation. Oystercatcher females also perform the 'whirring flight' possibly more frequently than the males, and this is probably the main means of finding a mate; Oystercatcher piping parties are now thought to be territorial in nature.

Once pair formation has taken place, the maintenance of the pair is aided in some species by means of specific ceremonies. In the Curlew, Redshank and Common Sandpiper (and probably several others) there is an alighting ceremony which follows the display flight (though it may be seen at other times, too). In these three species, the birds trill on set wings as they glide in to alight – on decurved wings in the Redshank and Sandpiper, and with raised wings in the Curlew – then, as they touch down, they pause with the wings held above the back, and continue to trill for a short time. Raising the wings vertically in this way is commonly seen in wading birds in general, at all times of the year. Sometimes it may have an aggressive function, but when performed by a pair as described above (a third bird may take part) it might well involve greeting and recognition elements.

Some waders will return to the breeding grounds already paired and it is possible that they have wintered together. When individuals arrive singly, they usually go about pair formation immediately. Occasionally this results in 'divorcees' when late arrivals find last year's mate already paired to another bird. Conclusive information of this type can only be derived from colour marking and few studies of this sort have been carried out. However, 'divorcees' may re-pair in the next breeding season. Some are inclined to retain a monogamous bond over a long period, others (of either sex) may take more than one mate and yet others, e.g. Pheasant-tailed Jacana and Painted Snipe, are polyandrous. Redshanks have been recorded as maintaining a pair for as long as seven years and sometimes a bond may last even longer. In the Ruff, however, pairing does not occur at all.

In the early breeding season, wing-lifting may give rise to a pre-copulatory display, particularly where this posture forms a part of courtship. In the Arctic, the whole series of behaviour patterns involved from pairing to laying is telescoped into a relatively short period and occurs clearly in sequence. In temperate areas, displays may take place five or six weeks before laying and are frequently incomplete as often the female is unco-operative through not having reached breeding condition. This can result in chases and fights which have been interpreted in the past as territorial behaviour but are merely a promiscuous male chasing an unco-operative female which will fight rather than allow copulation to take place. Sometimes males which are in breeding condition will display, and even attempt to copulate with, other males, and this has been recorded in Oystercatchers, Greenshanks and Redshanks. Probably this results from failure to recognize the sex and clearly in species where they are similar, little relevance can be placed on isolated observations of behaviour as indications of the sex of individuals.

Many wader species have developed the act of scraping out the nest into a display. This is most easily seen in the Plovers, which go down and rotate on the breast, using the feet to kick behind them fragments of soil and vegetation. Usually this is performed in the presence of the

Wood Sandpipers will contest territorial boundaries. These two birds have adopted an aggressive stance.

BELOW A Greenshank calls an alarm from a dead tree. Greenshanks are long-distance migrants and do not return to the breeding areas in Europe until April.

A Common Snipe displays as another bird (not shown) approaches.

OPPOSITE BELOW A Collared Pratincole adopting an aggressive posture.

BELOW Ringed Plovers defend a territory early in the breeding season; here a bird displays to itself in a mirror.

mate. The male makes the first depression, calling to the female and frequently fanning, elevating and depressing his tail with partially opened wings. The female enters the scrape and she too will kick out soil and vegetation as she rotates on her breast. Sandpipers also make scrapes, but since many of these nest in vegetation more than 10 cm (4 ins) deep, the display is difficult to observe. Here, too, the female is often present and in the excitement of the display will actually push the male out of the scrape, so that she can take his place. In this way numerous scrapes are made and Redshanks may produce up to fifteen early in the season. It is usual for the female to select one of these into which to deposit her first egg, and sometimes this may be on bare earth. Later only a single scrape may be produced, especially for replacement clutches.

In temperate areas it is far more usual to see attempted copulation than complete displays which lead to a successful coition. Within the group of wading birds, coition may be preceded by a variety of behaviour patterns ranging from practically none at all to the most elaborate courtships. Oystercatchers, for example, have little in the way of a pre-copulation ceremony and early in the season the males are extremely promiscuous, attempting coition with several different partners. In an established pair there may be no preliminaries and copulation may take place at almost any time. In a feeding pair the male may

ABOVE A Kittlitz's Plover, wing stretching.

ABOVE LEFT A Lapwing raises its wings. Many species of waders use this posture in threat display.

run up to the female, calling, and if she stops and tilts forward slightly, he will mount immediately. On other occasions the male will approach beating his wings vertically in much the same way as a male Greenshank or Redshank. Here is a courtship quite beautiful to watch, and one obviously entirely dependent upon the mood of the female.

This courtship can be initiated immediately following the alighting ceremony, by adopting the posture where the wings are raised and the birds are trilling, or it may follow scraping or arise from a situation in which both birds may be feeding or preening. The male bird begins to trill and lifts his wings vertically above his back, vibrating them and approaching the female in a crab-wise motion, partially sideways, with a high-stepping gait. Often the male will fan his tail and if the female is willing to co-operate she may herself sing, point her bill towards the ground and tilt slightly forward. When the male is immediately behind her his song changes to a low rattle where the bill is rapidly vibrated, though the note is still vocal. He beats his wings more rapidly, rises into the air and settles on the back of the female. He may remain there for a half minute, rattling, and still vibrating his vertically-held wings with which he maintains his balance. Then he flutters off and both birds may move away, apparently feeding, or merely pecking at grass blades. Similar ceremonies occur in other Sandpipers and the full pattern is both dramatic and beautiful.

An Avocet lifting its wings not in display but to settle its plumage.

74

If there is one thing more striking than the courtship of a pair of Sandpipers in the world of wading birds, it is the communal displays at the 'leks' of the Ruff and Great Snipe. These are assemblages of males which come together to attract females to their midst and, like moths to a lamp, they come. At the site of the lek there is a number of bare patches of earth each one some 30 cm (12 ins) in diameter, and the result of a Ruff's activity on that spot. These are called residences, and each is sited a metre (yard) or so from the next. The hierarchy within the lek is complex. Occupying these patches are resident males and on the edge of the lek are the marginal males; collectively these two groupings are known as independent males. Young males first coming to a lek, start off as marginal males, move in to the residences in subsequent years and in old age return to the periphery. Usually all these independent males are dark in colour (dark ruffs and ear tufts) though a few may be white. Satellite (immature) males which come into the lek are usually white, but a few have coloured ear tufts. They do not possess their own residences but their presence is tolerated by the independent males. Their function is to attract females (Reeves) to the lek. Like marginal males they move to the centre of the lek as they grow older. The Reeves may visit more than one lek and may copulate with more than one resident Ruff, even within the space of a few minutes. Satellite males copulate less frequently and usually when the resident cock is away

ABOVE A female Avocet defends her eggs.

OPPOSITE ABOVE A Ruff stretching its wings to re-arrange its feathers.

Injury feigning is common in many waders, and particularly in Plovers. It occurs most frequently at the time of the hatch, or when the chicks are only a few days old. Dotterels (LEFT) and Ringed Plovers (RIGHT) shown here are frequent performers of this distraction display.

PAGES 78–9 Avocets 'change over' during the incubation of the eggs.

76

chasing a rival. A resident male may have more than one satellite on his residence.

When a Reeve arrives the male usually crouches with his tail pointing towards her. The satellite male faces towards the female, but is usually chased off before the resident male attempts copulation.

Ruffs may display at leks several miles apart and it is interesting to follow the activities of individuals, which can be easily recognized by differences in ruff colour and ear tufts. It is less easy to follow the pattern of activity in Great Snipes, for this species leks at dusk and often far into the night. Again females are attracted to the displaying males, and like Ruffs, Great Snipes may lek in different places, up to 6 miles apart. Henry Seebohm, in his *Birds of Siberia*, recorded his good fortune in finding a lek inside the Arctic Circle where he was able to see the display by the light of the midnight sun. He described the males as stretching their necks and tilting back their heads until they almost touched the back and then rattling the bill in this peculiar posture to give a note like 'running one's finger along a comb'.

Another wader which displays at night is the Woodcock. It performs owl-like flights along woodland rides or just over the tree tops at dusk and dawn, an activity known as roding. The wing beats are much slower than in normal flight and every now and then the roding male utters a tri-syllabic call which can only be described as a croak. Some authorities have regarded roding as territorial in function but it is more likely to be an advertisement flight which stimulates the female to call down the flying male. Once on the ground copulation may follow immediately but in some instances there is a ground display where the male struts round the female, his tail fanned and raised and wings drooping.

Perhaps the best-known displays of wading birds are the distraction displays which are performed when young or hatching eggs are present. Injury feigning has obviously evolved to lead potential predators away from the nest or chicks. Strangely, not all individuals of a species will perform. Most Plovers will trail a wing and some will stumble and flop to the ground as they move away from the nest. Sometimes injury feigning is indulged in as a communal display. Some Pratincoles will surround a potential predator, adopting all sorts of postures, if the nest of one is threatened, and Pied (Black-winged) Stilts will collapse as though dead in groups well away from the nest, but performances from single birds are almost invariably associated with the eggs or young. The Killdeer Plover is said to increase the intensity of injury feigning as incubation proceeds and the habit is also common in Sandpipers – Dunlin, Curlew, Purple Sandpiper, Knot and Reeve are amongst the best performers. Reeves will jump into the air, as though attempting to fly, and fall to the ground with trailing wings.

Elements of courtship display are often involved in distraction of

Ringed Plovers take turns at incubating and the change over often involves one bird almost pushing the other off the nest.

Ruffs displaying at a lek; the residences are occupied by resident males, and satellite males (white collars) help to attract Reeves to the lek.

80

ABOVE A Greenshank crouching at the approach of a potential predator.

OPPOSITE Stone Curlews. The cock hunts for food on the ground for the newly hatched chick while the hen continues to incubate the second egg.

predators, particularly the 'butterfly' flight of the Oystercatcher and the display flight of the Redshank which is then performed very much lower (only 3–4 m (10–13 ft) above the ground) than it is in the early breeding season. Many habits that waders possess are used outside their normal context. Such 'displacement activities' include false feeding, false preening and picking up small stones and pieces of vegetation and throwing them away. These are habits een most frequently in stress situations, when false brooding might occur in some species, particularly Oystercatchers.

Waders are always doing something interesting and especially during the breeding season their displays attract attention. For those interested in breeding behaviour waders have the particular attraction of frequently performing in the open. There is still plenty to be discovered and if you are prepared to spend time watching and waiting your patience will be rewarded.

Nests, Eggs and Young

At best, the nests of waders are poor things compared with those made by many other birds. Nearly all species of wading birds nest on the ground, though some, such as Solitary Sandpipers, Green Sandpipers and sometimes Wood Sandpipers, will take over the disused nests of Passerines, built in trees, and use them as a platform for their eggs. Many 'nests' are merely depressions in the ground which, as we have seen, are excavated to some extent by the birds before the eggs are laid. Unused scrapes are often referred to as 'false nests', and many male birds will spend quite some time in a favourite, well-excavated scrape which may not eventually be selected by the female for laying. This can often be recognized by the presence of a pellet close by or even in the scrape itself.

Waders will often begin lining the scrape before laying. Pieces of vegetation or other surrounding materials, such as pebbles, are idly pulled into or placed around the scrape. The majority of the construction is carried out whilst the bird actually sits in the scrape, so initially all the material gathered will be from the immediate vicinity.

Some Oystercatchers will lay in a completely bare scrape but others collect large numbers of shells in and around the nest cup; this may even happen on saltmarsh, which means that sometimes the shells are deliberately carried to the nest. In such a terrain a shell-lined nest will be very obvious. Other beach-nesting waders use shells, or pieces of them, to help camouflage the nest.

In Sandpipers, which nest in vegetation, the amount of nest material is sometimes quite large and seems to depend on two factors: the possibility of flooding, and the availability and proximity of material. Stilts will increase the nest size in flood conditions and most Sandpipers will continue to bolster the nest throughout incubation.

The eggs of all waders are well marked, with the exception of those of the hole-nesting Crab Plover which are white. They vary in ground colour from yellowish cream to dark brown and are either spotted or blotched in various shades of olive, brown, grey and black. Even though

85

Sandpiper eggs may be hidden by a bower of vegetation, the eggs retain the dark coloration and patterning which matches their surroundings so well. Sand Plovers (and Ringed Plovers) have speckled eggs which are difficult to see on sand and gravel and Oystercatchers' eggs are very pebble-like. Plovers' eggs tend to be more boldly marked and blend in with short background vegetation, and the ashy eggs of Woodcock are very difficult to see on leaf-covered woodland floors. Snipes lay some of the darkest eggs and these tone in with small patches of standing water in marshy situations. Stone Curlews' eggs are often similar to those of Oystercatchers and are laid in very open and often arid situations where they look like rounded stones. Perhaps the most attractive eggs are those of the Jacanas; these have a high gloss and many are beautifully scrolled.

Whilst most waders rely on the colour of the eggs to provide sufficient camouflage, some species actively cover their eggs when they leave the nest: a brooding Kittlitz's Plover kicks sand over its eggs and the Least Seed Snipe scrapes dry earth over its nest before leaving.

Most waders lay pear-shaped eggs (pyriform), so the normal clutch of four fits snugly into the nest and occupies a relatively small area. This is important because waders tend to lay large eggs, and if more than four are laid the brooding bird will have great difficulty in covering them. However, there are several species which can hatch five or six eggs.

Nests and eggs of Lapwing (BELOW), Dotterel (OPPOSITE, ABOVE) and Little Ringed Plover.

CLOCKWISE FROM BOTTOM LEFT Nests and eggs of Pratincole, Cream-coloured Courser, Curlew, Woodcock and Redshank.

ABOVE LEFT Redshank nesting in deep vegetation.

Where fewer than four eggs make up the normal clutch, they are much more rounded and this is particularly the case in Stone Curlews and Pratincoles.

Birds tend to have a clutch size related to the optimal number of young which the adults can tend, and in waders which feed their young – Stone Curlews, Oystercatchers, Pratincoles, Sheathbills and Crab Plovers – the clutches are smaller than the probable ancestral four eggs. Some Snipes, which lay four eggs, feed their young for a few days, but largely, waders laying four eggs fend for themselves from hatching. There is a distinct tendency for Arctic waders to lay clutches of four, and in general smaller clutches occur towards the equator. All southern hemisphere Sandpipers lay fewer than four eggs and the clutch size is probably determined by food availability and mortality resulting from migration.

Most waders are capable of laying more eggs within a season than they do. Several species are double-brooded, i.e. having reared one family, the female will lay again and the pair rears a second lot of chicks. Snipes, Woodcocks, Ringed Plovers, Oystercatchers, Stone Curlews and Dunlins often behave in this way and there are records of Redshanks laying two clutches. It is commonplace for lost clutches to be replaced and a monogamous female may lay twelve or more eggs in a season because of this. Less common, but perhaps more interesting, is the

90

In the Kentish (Snowy) Plover the incubation is shared between the female (OPPOSITE RIGHT) and male (ABOVE).

situation where a female lays two clutches within a few days, one to be brooded by herself and the other by her mate. This happens in at least some populations of Temminck's Stint and Purple Sandpiper. Again, this habit appears to be commoner in the more northerly latitudes.

In most waders there is an interval of 30–46 hours between egg laying, but sometimes the period is much longer, particularly in bad weather. Often first eggs are lost to predators and in these circumstances the female puts off laying a second until another scrape is produced, and then she may produce a full clutch of four, or sometimes only three. In Sandpipers, which hide their eggs in vegetation, the first egg is often left exposed and vegetation not pulled over the nest until the second or third egg is laid. When a clutch is lost, its replacement may be started within three or four days, though ten days to a fortnight is more usual. In these circumstances 'divorce' might occur and a new mate be found, but there appears to be no difficulty in producing more eggs, despite their large size.

Eggs do not vary in size directly with the size of the female in wading birds. Common and Spotted Sandpipers may produce a clutch of four eggs which exceeds the weight of the female laying it, and Temminck's Stint, in laying two clutches, produces eggs which weigh 1.8 times the weight of the laying hen. At the other end of the scale, Curlew and Woodcock eggs are each only about 10 per cent of the weight of the

OPPOSITE Oystercatcher at the nest.

LEFT Stone Curlew turning the eggs during incubation.

BELOW The male Dotterel usually incubates the eggs.

Ringed Plover with young; the chicks dry out within an hour or two of hatching and are soon led from the nest.

female so that the whole clutch is only 40 per cent of the body weight.

Laying a clutch of four eggs normally takes about five or six days, and it is not until the last egg is laid that incubation begins. Where incubation is shared the eggs are usually brooded for more than 90 per cent of the time, but it is not unusual for both birds of a pair to be absent from the nest. As incubation progresses the eggs tend to be covered for longer periods. In species where male and female incubate separate clutches, brooding tends to be less complete and in Sanderlings behaving in this way, eggs tend to be covered for less than 75 per cent of the time.

Oystercatchers do not normally breed until they are three or four years of age whereas many of the smaller species are capable of breeding in their first year. Dunlins, Temminck's Stints and Redshanks have all been recorded breeding as first-year birds, and in the last-named species a female was sitting on a clutch of four eggs only ten months after she herself hatched.

Nearly all waders need to incubate but the Egyptian Plover may have to shield her eggs from the heat of the sun by standing over them, and on occasion she will bury them in the sand. Within the group all possible incubating regimes occur: in the Red-necked Phalarope the male incubates, whereas in the Ruff, the female (Reeve) is responsible for the whole of the breeding schedule. Most species share incubation though in some one sex takes the major role, the female, for example, in

OPPOSITE BELOW Killdeer Plover and chicks; all wader young are difficult to find once they have left the nest.

BELOW A Whimbrel chick appears anxious to be brooded.

the Oystercatcher. Often the non-incubating bird remains in the vicinity of the nest, particularly near hatching time, but on other occasions it may forage farther afield. There is usually some slight weight loss during incubation and even in Oystercatchers, which gain weight in winter when all other species are losing it, some is lost in the initial stages of incubation.

In the larger species, such as the Curlew, the incubation period lasts from 26–30 days but may be as short as 17 days in the smaller Red-necked Phalarope. Most species incubate for 22–24 days so that a nest is occupied, on average, for approximately 30 days, if the incubation proceeds normally. Hatching success varies enormously but it is usually in the range of 66–96 per cent. Ground-nesting birds are particularly vulnerable to predation and in temperate regions nests on grazing land may be trampled by cattle. In saltmarsh areas they are subject to inundation by the tide. Sometimes eggs are infertile, or become addled as a result of chilling and on occasions chicks have difficulty in emerging successfully. Some waders enjoy very high hatching success but this varies in different populations of the same species and also there is annual variation. Once hatched wader chicks must spend several weeks avoiding ground predators before they are able to fly. The nesting season is clearly a time of high mortality.

The majority of young leave the nest within twenty-four hours of hatching, but in Oystercatchers some may remain for two or three days and are fed by the adults. Waders' eggs which fail to hatch in the normal time are deserted and the adult birds lead the hatched chicks to suitable feeding areas. These might be quite some distance from the nest and the young will have to walk there, coached and encouraged by the parent birds. Where obstacles are encountered, the adults will carry the chicks over them, one at a time. The young birds are gripped between the parent's legs and pressed up against the belly. The first observations of this habit, seen in the Woodcock in the last century, were doubted, but it has since been witnessed in other species. Where the chicks are able to run or swim, they are allowed to do so, and carrying is only resorted to when necessary.

For two or three days after hatching, chicks lose weight but by the fourth day they have usually regained their birth weight. For the first two weeks or so the chicks are regularly brooded, for at this age they are unable to maintain their own body temperature. Once they are able to do this brooding becomes less frequent and towards the end of the fledging period one parent may desert the family. This happens particularly in Arctic breeders, where in Curlew Sandpipers and Pectoral Sandpipers the female alone tends the chicks, whereas in Dotterels and Phalaropes it is the male. In Phalaropes even the male often deserts the chicks before they can fly, so that for the last few days of the fledging

OPPOSITE The Black-winged Stilt often builds up its nest if flooding threatens.

BELOW The eggs of the Grey or Black-bellied Plover are difficult to see against the background of Canadian tundra vegetation.

96

The female Temminck's Stint often lays two clutches, one of which is brooded by the hen whilst the other is incubated by the male.

LEFT A Greater Sand Plover approaches her eggs in a Jordanian desert habitat.

A Greenshank about to settle onto her eggs in a typical Scottish Highland habitat.

period they fend entirely for themselves. In most species of waders, the chicks have found their own food supplies throughout this period, and the departure of one adult may well make more food available to them. In the high Arctic the chicks are entirely dependent upon the hatch of insects, and take a very high proportion of these. In fact in Alaska the period of emergence of crane flies is determined by the wader families. Early-hatching insects are snapped up by the various birds, and it is only when the insects emerge faster than they can be eaten that they are able to establish the next generation. Both larvae and adults of non-biting midges are also valuable food organisms for waders in this habitat. Farther south, in temperate regions, other insects become important. Not until after a chick has flown and left the nesting area does its bill achieve the adult length, and even young Sandpipers are obliged to pick organisms from the ground surface for much of the fledging period.

The time taken from hatching to the first flight varies with the different species. Phalaropes are the quickest – about 18–20 days – and Curlews and Oystercatchers take the longest – in some cases up to six weeks. However, most waders are able to fly by the time they have reached four weeks of age. At this stage they will not yet have gained their adult weight, nor are their wings fully developed because the primaries are still growing. These first flight feathers are retained normally until the autumn of the following year, so in many cases they

99

last some fifteen months. Many of the juvenile body feathers, which replace the down, are shed in the first autumn when the first winter plumage is acquired, but tail feathers, some tertiaries and wing coverts are retained until the first spring of life when most waders obtain a breeding plumage.

Very little is known about the mortality of chicks during the fledging period because they are so difficult to trace, and the fact that only one or two chicks of a brood can be found does not mean that others are not alive. The brood often scatters when adults give warning and young chicks are very hard to spot. Sometimes family parties can be seen shortly after the young have fledged but it is only in populations of marked birds that any idea of the number of young which have survived to fly can be estimated. Estimates of fledging success vary greatly, even within a species. In the Oystercatcher, differences ranging from 4.6–86 per cent have been quoted. Generally, projections vary between 40 per cent and 80 per cent, but most of these are probably underestimates as it is easy to overlook chicks.

Obviously, chicks are very susceptible to predation before they can fly and at this time the adult birds usually defend an area around them against potential predators. Defence is usually limited to mobbing and the use of alarm calls and sometimes mobbing becomes communal. Groups of waders numbering up to twenty, from quite a wide area (as

OPPOSITE The Woodcock is almost invisible on the woodland floor as she incubates her eggs.

BELOW The eggs of the Wood Sandpiper are large in comparison with the bird and the incubating female appears only just able to cover them.

ABOVE A Western Sandpiper arranges her eggs before settling on them.

ABOVE RIGHT The Purple Sandpiper melts into the background of the tundra vegetation during incubation.

OPPOSITE ABOVE A Reeve negotiating deep vegetation in the approach to the nest. Like Redshanks, Reeves conceal their eggs well.

OPPOSITE A pair of Terek Sandpipers at the nest. Photographed in Finland.

much as 400–500 m/yards in radius) may collectively mob mammalian predators, but the approach of crows and raptors is generally signalled by an adult using an alarm note; most chicks crouch, concealed in vegetation, during such behaviour. When a predator comes in close, the parent birds may resort to diversionary tactics, such as low display flights or injury feigning, but such distractions are often to no avail. Chicks are also particularly subject to chilling, especially during cold, wet weather, and in saltmarsh areas some drown despite the fact that they are able to swim.

On hatching, the chicks are covered in down and each species has a characteristic pattern of dark markings on the dorsal side and on the flanks. This serves to break up the outline and makes them difficult to see (provided they remain immobile) even when they are not covered by vegetation. The patterning is similar within each group of waders and it has been used as a basis for suggesting possible lines of evolution. Down remains amongst the body feathers until well after fledging but the pattern of markings begins to change as soon as contour feathers sprout.

At the end of the breeding season young birds and their parents often separate and may well move to different wintering areas. For some months the juveniles suffer a higher mortality than the adults but even so at the end of the fledging period a wader population may be

103

ABOVE Grey Phalarope about to settle on its eggs.

ABOVE LEFT Common Sandpiper brooding newly hatched chicks. The egg tooth, used to break out of the egg, is still present on the bill of the downy chick.

LEFT A young Ruff ventures into the water.

OPPOSITE Curlew chick (TOP); Whimbrel chick (BOTTOM).

numerically two to three times greater than it was in the spring. Often juveniles (birds of the year) can be identified in post-breeding flocks and if so it is possible to estimate the success of the previous breeding season. All wader populations suffer good and bad seasons, but a high proportion of juveniles in an autumn flock is indicative of a good one.

Once the chicks have flown, any adults remaining on the breeding areas soon move off. The return to the shore is not long delayed and both adults and young of most species turn once again to the marine invertebrates for sustenance. The breeding season is relatively short, but a great deal of energy is put in to getting to the nesting grounds, rearing chicks and returning to the wintering area each year. Clearly it is worth all the effort involved or the birds would adopt a different strategy, but as the season ends, yet more energy is needed to ensure a successful moult. Some waders, e.g. Alaskan Dunlins, begin the moult on the breeding ground, but most species do not moult until they reach an intermediate staging post or the wintering quarters. Here they put on weight in preparation for the winter, an insurance policy against a time when food is, perhaps, unavailable. Clouds of waders again frequent the southern mudflats where the various marine food items have increased in numbers during the temporary absence of their predators. Only a few birds will have summered here – immature and older waders whose physiology has condemned them to a temperate summer. Now the countless hordes return, a myriad probing, pecking bills to reap the rich harvest from the mud, a feast indeed for young waders which were beginning to find Arctic insects hard to find.

Seasonal Movements

The high summer of the northern hemisphere is a time of relative inactivity for most birds, and the coastlines of temperate regions harbour only a few waders which were not in a physiological state for breeding in the spring. As autumn approaches their numbers increase as birds move south from their Arctic breeding grounds and suddenly the mud flats and estuaries are alive with a myriad birds. At high tide they fall into roosts like so much confetti and demonstrate incredible manoeuvrability as they twist and turn in immense flocks that catch the autumn sunlight. In some places they stay only fleetingly, moving to warmer areas to winter; in others they stay to moult, and in some they remain for the winter.

At this time there is something for everyone interested in birds. For many the sight of such large gatherings is an attraction in itself; for others the search for rarities is the main appeal. In their southerly migration small numbers of birds fail to follow the ancient routes or are driven off course by vagaries of the climate, and these are avidly sought by the rarity hunters. For the most part the migrants follow time-honoured paths and whilst many perish on the way, more survive than would do so were they to remain on the breeding grounds. It is because of this that the migratory habit has evolved. Migrants' movements are determined by the location of their food supplies and often this necessitates immense journeys to places where food is assured for the winter season. Many species of wading birds are truly globe-trotters and cover distances far greater than those of most other birds. The record in this respect is probably held by the White-rumped Sandpiper which travels up to 9,000 miles twice each year between Alaska and Tierra del Fuego. Almost as spectacular are the movements of the American (Lesser) Golden Plover, which nests on the tundra of northern Canada and winters on the pampas of South America, an annual round trip in excess of 15,000 miles. Whilst that in itself is a considerable feat, the fact that the journey south in autumn involves a non-stop sea crossing from Labrador to Surinam or the north coast of Brazil (some 2,400 miles) is even more remarkable.

ABOVE Sanderlings and a few Dunlins in flight. Waders tend to migrate in small groups.

OPPOSITE ABOVE Sanderlings roosting. This species is a long-distance migrant, and can cover 2000 miles of the Pacific without a stop.

OPPOSITE BELOW Knot in summer plumage. Birds which nest in north Greenland and Ellesmere Island cross the Greenland ice-cap into Europe in autumn; many arrive in full breeding plumage.

PAGE 108 A flock of Curlew Sandpipers on the East African coast. Birds which nest on the Taimyr Peninsula are capable of crossing the Sahara non-stop.

For a land bird to achieve such a crossing might suggest that a little help is involved. Indeed it is, for these Plovers have evolved the direction of their migratory flights to take advantage of the prevailing winds. From Canada these blow eastwards, and as the birds tend to begin their autumn journey in a south-easterly direction, they are, in effect, wind-assisted. In spring the birds make use of the westerly winds in Brazil and set off north-north-west on a route which takes them over the land bridge between North and South America. Whilst the direction of these spring and autumn flights can be observed in the field, it is interesting that laboratory experiments have also shown this difference in direction selection on the two journeys, captive Plovers showing a tendency to move north-north-west in spring and south-east in autumn. This elliptical journey is also made by other species which take similar advantage of the winds.

Migratory flights are fuelled by fat deposition prior to take-off and recent calculations suggest that the crossing from Canada to South America would require some 18g (0.6 oz) of fat, significantly less than was once thought to be needed. Whilst birds making this journey could rest on islands en route, this would not be possible on flights from the Aleutians to Hawaii and Wake Island, which is half way between the Aleutians and New Guinea. On Wake Island birds arrive with over 20g

(0.7 oz) of unburned fat and it has been calculated that the American Golden Plovers may have a flight range of 6,200 miles in spring and 5,900 miles in autumn. A non-stop flight from the Aleutians to Hawaii would take 35 hours, involve 252,000 wing beats and be carried out at an average speed of 45 mph!

It is clear, too, that other species of waders are perfectly capable of covering 2,500 miles of ocean, almost certainly non-stop, as Turnstones, Wandering Tattlers, Dunlins, Sanderlings, Greater Yellowlegs and Snipes are amongst species recorded on Wake Island in winter. Siberian Arctic breeding species such as Bristle-thighed Curlews, Bar-tailed Godwits and Knots winter as far south as Australia and New Zealand – so their journeyings are truly global.

Just as the oceans are no barrier to many species of migrating waders, so ice-caps and deserts are traversed with equal ease. Knots, which occur in such numbers on western European coasts, cross the Greenland ice-cap each spring and autumn to and from their nesting sites in Ellesmere Island (Canada). Though many may rest in Iceland, others surely make the crossing from Greenland, and possibly the entire journey, non-stop. Recent calculations suggest they have the capability to accomplish this. Siberian Knots winter farther south, in Africa, and make the flight on great-circle routes, so carrying out the journey most efficiently in using the minimum of energy. In the same way, Curlew Sandpipers, which nest in the Taimyr Peninsula (northern Siberia), cross the Sahara non-stop and at considerable heights, so they may be capable of negotiating the additional hazard of the Mediterranean Sea before re-fuelling in the region of the Black Sea.

Much of our knowledge of the migration of waders comes from watching visible migration, mainly the arrival and departure of birds, from known vantage points, but two other sources of information are important: ringing or banding; and radar studies. Ringing provides information about wintering areas and, to some extent, migration routes, whereas the use of radar has afforded new facts about the height, speed, timing and direction of movement. Each method alone has its limitations; most migration is not visible, ringing provides information only from those areas where recoveries are possible and in radar studies identification of species is often difficult and low movements impossible to observe. Together they give us an overall picture of what happens.

Most wader movement takes place between 500m and 3,000m (1500 ft and 10,000 ft) above sea-level but Godwits and Curlews have been recorded at more than twice this height in the Himalayas. In rain waders fly close to the surface of the sea but generally select altitudes at which wind conditions are favourable. The speed of migratory flight tends to be slightly faster than normal flight and in many cases species can be identified through the speed of their movements on radar screens. Most

112

The Marbled Godwit breeds in the prairie provinces of Canada and migrates south to Guatemala and South America.

OPPOSITE BELOW The Long-billed Curlew migrates south from breeding areas in western Canada to winter as far south as Guatemala.

BELOW Spotted Redshank in summer plumage. Some species move south singly and sometimes arrive in full breeding plumage.

wader species migrate more slowly than the American Golden Plover, at between 40 mph and 50 mph.

The vast autumn flocks result from the coming together of smaller migratory parties; waders tend to migrate in groups of a few hundred individuals at most. The Eskimo Curlew was recorded in the last century as 'travelling by the millions' and perhaps this was an exception. There can be little doubt that, huge though the flocks may have been, they were usually to be numbered in thousands rather than millions.

Not all wader migration takes the form of extensive spring and autumn movements. Some species are sedentary and others move short distances but one factor which radar studies have brought to the fore is that migration takes place in all months of the year. The autumn drift southwards begins in many species before the northerly spring movement is completed in the high Arctic forms, and movements occur throughout the winter, often in response to cold snaps and the unavailability of food. In Europe cold weather results in Lapwings from the Continent crossing the North Sea to the British Isles and the British population moving into Ireland or south to Spain. As the weather improves Lapwings move back to the Continent so that throughout the winter there is a regular 'shuttle service' across the North Sea. Obviously these flights use up a lot of energy, but it must be available to

ABOVE Wintering flocks of Lapwings often move into Ireland during cold spells when other flocks arrive in England from the Continent.

the birds in the form of food reserves for them to carry out these journeys which are clearly, from their point of view, worthwhile.

In looking at migratory waders it is difficult not to speculate from where they might have come. Greenshanks resting by a lakeside in Kenya might well have been in northern Scandinavia or Siberia a few days previously and it is easy to understand the interest and excitement engendered in ringers by long-distance recoveries. The casual bird-watcher might see a ringed bird but know nothing of its history. However, with the advent of colour-dying and of marking birds with wing tags, he can play an important part in our search for knowledge of wader movements. Any observation anywhere in the world of a colour-marked bird, reported to the British Trust for Ornithology, at Tring in Hertfordshire, England, will almost certainly result in the observers being informed of when and where the bird was marked. Birds colour-marked in Greenland were observed much more frequently than was ever expected in Great Britain, and such sightings can add greatly to a day's birdwatching.

Whilst many species of waders are amongst the greatest globe-trotters of the bird world, others are relative home-lovers and breed and winter in much the same area. Even within a single species different populations behave in different ways. Ringed Plovers nesting in Greenland leap-frog over the populations of Britain and southern Scandinavia

PAGES 116–17 Sanderlings alight on an outcrop of sandstone on the Dee estuary – a refuge at high tide.

115

and winter in south-west Africa; northern Scandinavian Ringed Plovers behave similarly. The northernmost nesting Redshank winter in Africa, farther south than others, and, in some cases, populations are kept as separate in winter as they are during the breeding season. Different populations of the same species are able to react to environmental stresses and quickly evolve behavioural responses which result in the largest number of individuals surviving. This is usually brought about by a small proportion of a population being genetically different from the rest and, consequently, they may be favoured by environmental changes. This is seen most easily in the relation of moult to migration. Most long-distance waders moult after the migration, or at staging posts during it. Again, a small proportion of each population behaves differently. If it becomes advantageous to moult before migrating this can be quickly selected for, as has been the case in Alaskan-breeding Dunlin (Red-backed Sandpiper) from Point Barrow. This population begins the autumn moult almost as soon as birds arrive on the breeding ground, whereas Dunlin from northern Scandinavia do not shed their feathers until they arrive on their wintering grounds in North Africa.

Waders, like other birds, are able to respond quickly to environmental pressures and this can be clearly seen in the changing patterns of movements which must have occurred as a result of the ice ages. During the past million years (the Pleistocene) ice has moved south from the

OPPOSITE Two North American waders which occasionally arrive on European shores: the Least Sandpiper (ABOVE) and the Solitary Sandpiper (BELOW).

BELOW During migration in rainy conditions waders often hug the water surface. This group of Oystercatchers includes a Curlew and an immature Herring Gull.

ABOVE Redshanks at high tide. Amongst these birds photographed on the Cheshire Dee are many which have moved south from Iceland.

OPPOSITE The North American Willet is another wader which has now occurred in Europe.

high Arctic into southern Europe and North America on at least four major occasions and pushed the waders and other birds south. As the ice retreated so the areas uncovered were recolonized and many of the great migration routes now follow the paths of the retreating ice. When refuges for tundra-nesting waders occurred only in Alaska, Verkhoyansk (north-east Siberia) and Greenland, it was from the last that Europe was colonized. Now we have the great Knot flyways across the Greenland ice-cap leading into Europe for winter and channelling the return in spring. Each winter the push south is a tiny reflection of what happened during each major ice age, though, of course, many other factors are now involved.

Changing day length affects the physiology of birds to bring them into migratory condition, in which they show a general restlessness. Temperature and weather variations may also stimulate movements, though cold snaps may result in a return. Once the migration has begun, birds are able to orientate, using their built-in 'clocks', in relation to the sun during the day and the star patterns at night. Waders are able to navigate accurately in overcast conditions and can compensate for drift by the wind but it is not easy to explain how young unaccompanied birds manage to find their way to the traditional wintering grounds. American Golden Plovers tend to move south before their young so that the latter make the 8,000 mile journey to South America unassisted and

121

without previous experience. They may well have an inherited capacity to fly in a standard direction for a specific time, and there is experimental evidence to support this suggestion.

Occasionally some birds miss their way or are driven off course by bad weather. As a result, North American waders turn up every year in Europe and provide exciting watching in such vantage points as the Scilly Isles, for those interested in rarities. Conversely European birds sometimes go in the opposite direction and there are records of Lapwings, obviously heading for Ireland, completely missing it and ending up in Newfoundland. In 1927 one of these Lapwings was a British-ringed bird. Perhaps one of the most unusual records was that of a British birdwatcher on his first visit to the Seychelles encountering a Little Curlew, a close relative of the Eskimo Curlew, over 2,000 miles from its nearest normal wintering area in eastern Indonesia.

The regular occurrence of birds away from their normal wintering areas may well indicate changes in climate or behaviour. This may be the case with North American wader vagrants in Europe which are now seen much more commonly than they were twenty-five years ago. This is probably not merely a case of more birdwatchers as there has not been a similar increase in the sightings of rare Eurasian waders.

Before migrating most waders build up their fat reserves but in spring these might not be solely to fuel the journey. In some cases reserves

Redshanks and Turnstones. The Redshank on the right was ringed as a chick on the Ribble Marshes National Nature Reserve by W. G. Hale.

Siberian waders occasionally stray to the British Isles; this Sharp-tailed Sandpiper is a rare visitor.

RIGHT Lapwings moving west in autumn are occasionally driven across the Atlantic and reach North America.

might be needed by high Arctic birds on arrival at the breeding grounds, and often staging posts are used to build up these reserves. Many estuaries act in this way and are essential world-wide for maintaining wader populations. From the Copper River Delta in Alaska to the Dutch Waddensee and estuaries such as the Cheshire Dee in Britain, staging posts form an essential part of the migration system. They provide food and often a place in which to moult.

In our conservation of wetlands it is essential to protect those areas which accommodate waders on passage. An estuary with only relatively small numbers at any one time may well have a large through-put, and the loss of such an area could have far-reaching consequences on our wader populations. A more extensive knowledge of wader movements will help conservation strategies and go some way to ensure that our Knot flocks are not subject to the same fate as that of the Eskimo Curlew in the last century.

Probably no other group of birds contains such a number of globe-trotters as the waders. Their journeys cover most of the earth's surface but we see little of the actual movements. They usually occur too high to see, or at night, when perhaps they are a little more obvious as birds can often be heard calling to each other. Their most striking manifestation is the presence of vast flocks on mudflats which yesterday were quiet. These flocks are best seen at high tide when the flow pushes them onto exposed refuges where they rest after their flight, often in preparation for the continuation of their journeyings which will go on as long as the seasons change.

Flocking and Roosting

Waders can be seen in flocks at any time. In the spring some non-breeding birds remain away from the nesting areas, often on the shore, but it is in the autumn that waders come together in their largest numbers. Once breeding is over, small feeding parties form and migration usually takes place in flocks which are formed by several feeding groups coming together.

In the flock all the birds tend to behave in the same way at the same time. In some circumstances, such as when they are resting, some individuals may be doing different things but, in general, specific activities are synchronized – for example, if a flock takes flight, all the birds leave the ground at approximately the same time, and if the birds are feeding, usually all are moving forward in the same direction at the same speed. There is clearly a tendency for individuals to copy the reactions of others and, particularly in waders, to maintain a fixed distance from each other. The sudden exposure of wing flashes or the sound of alarm calls produce an instant response from the rest of the flock, and all react similarly even though they may have been indulging in rather different activities prior to the stimulus.

If waders are disturbed the birds tend to move closer to each other as they take flight, but they are always spaced farther apart when feeding. At their roost they will pack even more tightly than when flying. Each species seems to have evolved its own individual distance, and the species of the bird in question can often be recognized by the spatial distribution within the group. At roosts, Knots pack close, Dunlin produce looser aggregations, and Oystercatchers, Curlews and Godwits usually have several bird lengths between each other.

At low tide the waders are spread out over the mudflats, feeding in the wetter channels and avoiding the higher, drier banks. At this time the birds may be several metres (yards) apart. Sanderlings and Godwits are often straggled along the tide's edge and whilst single individuals of one species might be found amongst small flocks of another, the overall impression given by the feeding birds is that of a loose, single-species

127

flock. Many of these loose flocks follow the ebbing tide, feeding all the time, and as it turns so they are pushed back towards the shore. About three hours before the tide is at its height, Oystercatchers begin to lose interest in feeding and start to wend their way to the high-tide roost. They move in small groups at first, calling, towards their traditional roosting sites and this is the time when the larger estuaries begin to come alive. Throughout the period of low water the birds have fed far out on the flats and to the casual observer the estuary seems lifeless at this time. The flooding tide changes the silent marshes into a hive of activity, as more and more Oystercatchers begin to move and gather at sub-roosts on the inner mudflats. As they fly in from the tideline they are noisy, calling to each other in flight, and every now and then piping in unison from the ground. Some tuck their bills into their scapulars and, standing on one leg, apparently go to sleep, swaying from side to side to head the wind, only to be disturbed later by the tide. Even then, some leave their bills tucked away as they hop on one leg away from the advancing water. Eventually they may take flight and move to the final high-tide roost. Sub-roosts of Oystercatchers are common and other species form them on occasions. Only on the lowest tides do these constitute the final roosts.

The tidal cycles are such that once every two weeks, at the first and third quarters of the moon, the tides are highest (springs) and it is at these times that the birds will be found on the highest parts of the shore. At neap tides the birds remain farther out on the mud forming less dense roosts. On the highest spring tides they often move onto the saltmarsh and occasionally may be pushed off the saltings altogether.

No matter what the state of the tide the Oystercatchers arrive at the high-tide roost first and it is some time, perhaps an hour, before other waders move in. Grey Plovers, Godwits and Curlews are usually next to arrive. They are easy to recognize as they fly up the estuary, the Plovers whistling plaintively and the Godwits and Curlews strung out in straggling lines across the sky. The Godwits chatter continuously; a Curlew may add a trill to the whistles of its fellows. In the autumn, Godwits go in for 'crazy flying' and break from the normal flight to throw themselves about the sky. More and more birds move in to the roost, with Knots and Dunlins flying high and with the Godwits and Ringed Plovers scudding over the surface of the mud. Wave upon wave of birds all move in the same direction; all are calling; the marsh is teeming with sound and movement. Such is the activity that it is difficult to imagine where all the birds get to at low tide. At the roost itself myriads of waders circle in the air; Knots and Dunlins are usually in the majority and the clamour has to be heard to be believed. Most of the sound comes from the Godwits and Knots, but as they arrive Oystercatchers join in the calling. Above all can be heard the sound

OPPOSITE ABOVE The roost forming: Knots, Dunlins, Redshanks and Curlews begin to congregate at high tide.

OPPOSITE BELOW Oystercatchers and Curlews in the surf.

PAGE 126 Roosting waders, including Knots, Dunlins, Turnstones, Redshanks and Sanderlings.

of a multitude of wings, like a gale blowing through the forest edge.

As more birds arrive some on the ground will take off and move up spirally into the air, circle, then plunge to the flats whilst others come down slowly like snowflakes on a windless day. On the horizon moving 'smoke clouds' change shape as they approach, then suddenly the individual birds are resolved by the eye. Dramatically they catch the sun, tower in the sky, turn, glint, shimmer in the sunlight and then darken the sky as they cross the sun. Nothing could be designed more critically to catch the eye than these avian acrobats, the star performers of which are the Knots. With a rush of wings more Dunlins arrive and plane down into the roost where the different species are now beginning to arrange themselves in some sort of order as the tide nears its height. Most birds have now settled, though there is still movement on the ground and in the air, and the volume of sound is not so great.

As the tide flows the Godwits stand in the water, resting now after their aerial exertions, many with the bill turned into the feathers, sleeping. They ignore the water as it reaches almost to their bellies, but the Oystercatchers hop away up the beach where the Knots, with their much shorter legs, are massed like a grey carpet on the mud, out of reach of the water. Dunlins pack less tightly, again well above the high-water mark, and Grey Plovers are scattered amongst them. Curlews and Redshanks gather on the edge of the saltmarsh, the former

A group of Redshanks roosting at high tide.

130

Redshanks making their way to the roost.

often in deep vegetation such as *Spartina*. Ringed Plovers and Sanderlings mingle with the Dunlins, many of which continue feeding in pools on the flats, throughout the period of high tide. Most other species are now still and silent and from a distance the roost can only be seen as a greyish line on the shore, but from the air the picture is very different.

With the sun shining on the roost, the tightly packed Knot are visible from far above as a creamy mass in the dark mud, but where the sun catches the wet surface to be reflected back into the sky, the Knot appear black. From every angle they can be seen for miles! Even the less densely packed waders are easily seen but, surprisingly, Oystercatchers on the flats do not catch the eye from the air. On green saltmarsh Oystercatchers stand out, as indeed do all the other species when they roost there, but on the mud these black and white waders blend into the background. Most Sandpipers have pale underparts and brownish or greyish upper parts in winter and their coloration is generally supposed to afford camouflage on the shore. When birds occur singly, it does so, but in flocks it serves to attract attention at long range. This is not accidental, for the changing shape of flocks approaching and leaving the roost, the banking to catch the sun and the general obtrusiveness of the flock could all clearly have been selected against. In fact, waders could hardly be more obvious at roosts than they are. Selection has taken place to draw attention to their presence.

PAGES 132–3 Dunlins are spaced farther apart than Knots at the roost.

131

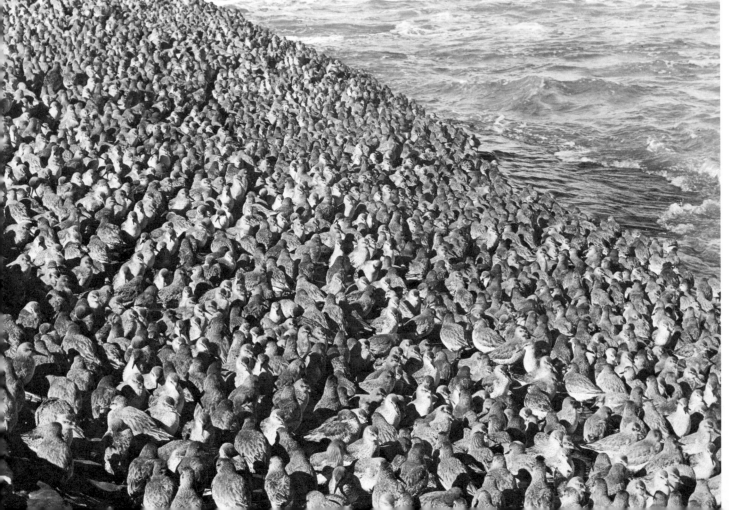

OPPOSITE ABOVE A Kentish (Snowy) Plover sheltering from the wind in a hollow in the sand.

OPPOSITE BELOW Knots pack more closely than any other species of wader. This flock of about 5000 is waiting for the tide to turn.

In the autumn roosting flocks, many birds preen their moulting feathers before sleeping and even the Dunlin may be inactive. Whilst they appear to be off their guard, this is not the case. At the appearance (real or imagined) of an avian predator they take off with a rush of wings, turn and twist in the air and again advertise their presence over a wide area. With the passing of the danger they settle again and are soon apparently asleep, but not for long. An hour after high tide all but the Oystercatchers show signs of activity, preening, bathing, stretching their wings and shuffling about in the flock. Dunlins begin to feed, small Plovers run about and Sanderlings like clockwork mice dart in and out of pools. Winter roosts are apt to be more lively as Dunlins feed over the period of the high tide and other small waders are often active then.

The ebbing tide leaves the mud glistening. With a rush of wings Dunlins and Sanderlings move down the shore and spread themselves out to feed. The Sanderlings make for the waterline where they dart in and out of the receding tide, feeding in much the same way as a Wagtail at a river's edge, picking at items washed in. More movement occurs in the Knot flock and with a crescendo of sound half the flock moves down the shore to form an active sub-roost on the wet mud. Birds at the back of the flock leap-frog over their neighbours and there is an obvious anxiety to return to feeding far out on the flats. Then, with an even

BELOW Grey or Black-bellied Plovers in winter plumage at high tide.

greater sound of rushing wings and vocal accompaniment, the rest of the small waders and the Knots, together with many Godwits and Grey Plovers, are in the air in a vast, mixed flock. Even a few enthusiastic Oystercatchers go with them, all flying low over the flats, all heading for the feeding grounds. And then silence.

On the roost the majority of the Oystercatchers are still sleeping and many Godwits remain. Some of the Godwits which left with the smaller Sandpipers form a temporary sub-roost on the flats, but soon leave to feed on the edge of the ebbing tide. Other Godwits join them, leaving only the Oystercatchers behind, apparently in no hurry to go cockling. For an hour or more they remain there. Apart from the odd Dyke Dunlin and a few noisy Redshanks they appear to be the only birds on the marsh, standing quietly above their reflections. Suddenly, and for no apparent reason, they are in the air forming long lines, straggling out low over the mudflats to be joined by those birds from the sub-roost which left the main roost earlier. Quietly they disappear into the distance where the cockle beds lie. The only traces of the roost are the thousands of footmarks, the white droppings blending into the mud, and the moulted feathers scattered across the surface. Numerous pellets can be found on close inspection but these will disappear at the next tide if it is higher or in the rain when it comes. There are no birds. The marsh is deserted. Where many thousands of waders had recently spent the hours of the high tide, there is stillness. It is little wonder that potential land developers are puzzled by our anxiety to preserve so wet and inhospitable a wilderness. Apparently nothing lives there and at this time perhaps they can be forgiven for thinking this way; the next high tide would give them a different perspective of this priceless wader refuge.

The positioning of the roost is important. It must be situated so that little disturbance occurs and a good roost is as important as a good feeding ground. In addition there must be suitable sites at all states of the tide and in some areas waders are prepared to travel in excess of 15 miles to reach their high-tide roost. Many favoured sites have been used since time immemorial and their loss can have serious repercussions on wintering wader populations.

On the Cheshire Dee, Hilbre Island and its associated islets once formed a classical roosting site which had existed for centuries. Disturbance of this area and other mainland roosts on the Dee has resulted in waders occasionally spending the whole of the high-tide period on the wing, spiralling up and gliding down over a period of two to three hours, landing only when the tide has receded sufficiently to allow them to occupy undisturbed areas of the mud. It is very interesting that the waders have enough energy to do this and it implies that, at least for these birds, the food supply is more than adequate.

The British Trust for Ornithology's *Birds of Estuaries Enquiry* revealed that nearly three million waders winter in western Europe, and just under a million in North Africa. Most of these were counted at roosts where the concentration of birds made this possible. It is unlikely that all roosts were included in the census, though in a highly populated area such as western Europe, most of the bigger ones would be found. Aerial surveys played an important role: apart from being able to follow flocks to the roosting sites, so discovering new ones in the exercise, it was also possible to photograph birds in two dimensions on the ground. In this way the accuracy of ground counts could be assessed by comparison with those made from aerial photographs.

Not all roosts occur on the shore. In many countries waders winter by freshwater lakes and some, including Plovers and Curlews, winter inland, where the birds congregate at dusk. Arrivals at these roosts are not so dramatic as they are in coastal areas, though 'crazy flying' is often a feature. Some species of waders will form communal roosts when they first arrive at the breeding areas, and noisy gatherings they are, too. Curlews usually give voice to full song when they arrive at the roost and this is often repeated by birds on the ground, even after dusk.

A particular feature of inland roosts is the fact that during the period of the full moon, waders will sleep during the day and feed at night. Lapwings and Golden Plovers feed as efficiently at night as during the

ABOVE Sanderlings alight at the roost.

OPPOSITE ABOVE Aerial view of the Ribble Marshes, Lancashire. Counting waders from the air is often easier than from the ground.

OPPOSITE BELOW Knots with Redshanks, Dunlins, Sanderlings and Oyster-catchers.

PAGE 136 Turnstones and Knots on Hilbre Island.

OPPOSITE ABOVE A Willet and a Whimbrel dispute a stand at high tide.

OPPOSITE BELOW A mixed species flock of waders leaves the roosting site as the tide recedes.

day, and there can be little doubt that Oystercatchers do so too. Whilst relatively little information exists, it would be surprising if other night feeders were not equally efficient. This activity has nothing to do with the additional light cast by a full moon, as waders will feed then when the sky is fully overcast. There is a rhythm to the feeding, possibly associated with a lunar periodicity in the activity of the prey, but little is yet known about this particularly interesting feature of wader ecology.

There can be no doubt that wader flocks actively advertise their presence – but why should they do this? If flocking was merely engaged in as an anti-predator measure it would surely pay the birds to attract as little attention to the flock as possible. The aerobatics of waders at the roost are very reminiscent of the behaviour of a flock in the presence of danger, and it was thought for some time that this device had evolved to confuse predators. However, it occurs much more frequently in their absence than it does in their presence and whilst the confusion element does exist, this pattern of activity almost certainly has more far-reaching effects. In some areas predators occur much more frequently than in others and in California up to 21 per cent of Dunlin and 16 per cent of Dowitchers are taken in this way in winter, so flocking and flock behaviour may well have a greater importance there than in western Europe. The most likely explanation for self-advertisement by wader flocks lies in the attraction of solitary birds and small groups which then learn the location of the best food supplies without having to seek it for themselves. Communal roosts probably act primarily as information centres and have a secondary function in defence against predators. Flocking is clearly very important to wading birds and in the management of our wetlands it must be ensured that good roosting sites are protected, for they play a crucial part in the ecology of wading birds.

RIGHT An aerial roost on the Cheshire Dee. At very high tides waders stay on the wing until the ebb; they may circle, spiralling up and gliding down, for two hours or more.

Dry-land Waders and Fresh-water Shorebirds

Not all waders are birds of cold regions nor are they all birds of the shore. Some species inhabit desert regions and many spend their entire lives inland. Others have evolved in ways which have left them looking little like their shore-living cousins, but they are still considered to be waders because they are related to the Plovers, Sandpipers and Oyster-catchers.

Stone Curlews, Coursers, Pratincoles and several species of Lapwings are mainly birds of drier habitats and of these only a few of the Lapwings and one or two of the Stone Curlews are regularly associated with wet places. Woodcocks, too, are birds of drier habitats, though they have a particular preference for the damp floors of woodlands.

There are, at present, nine species of Stone Curlews or Thick-knees: two in South America, three in Africa, two in Australasia and one each in the Palaearctic and Oriental regions. For waders they are large, and look like a cross between a Bustard and a Plover. In England the Stone Curlew was at one time known as the Norfolk Plover, but the Thick-knees are neither Curlews nor Plovers. No other waders are in any way like them. At close quarters, from a hide, their enormous, amber-coloured eyes have an almost hypnotic quality and the colloquial name 'goggle-eye' is more appropriate than the names in general use. The Great Stone Curlew, the largest species, is a bird of the Indian coastline and river beds, and the Beach Stone Curlew is found exclusively on the Australasian coast and in the Andaman and Solomon Islands. The Water Dikkop is another shore Thick-knee; the Senegal Thick-knee is also associated with water, though most other species are birds of drier areas. Their plumage blends into the background and the winter and summer plumages are similar. During the day they tend to remain inactive and seek the shelter of vegetation. In the evening, however, they become quite vocal, their mournful cries being heard most frequently during the breeding season and early in autumn. Calling often continues into the night, particularly when there is a moon.

Stone Curlews lay two eggs, which are rather like those of Oyster-

143

catchers, and the chicks are well camouflaged and difficult to find. At the end of the breeding season the European Stone Curlews form small flocks, which may contain family groups, and migrate south into southern Europe and North Africa. Most other species are relatively sedentary.

The Water Dikkop has an interesting association with crocodiles; it lays its eggs at the same time as they do and will brood them within a few feet of the reptiles. The latter's presence apparently affords the birds some degree of protection from egg predators, and possibly the Dikkops warn the reptiles of approaching danger, so there may well be a degree of mutualism in the relationship. The Dikkop is often referred to as a Crocodile Bird, but this term is more applicable to another wader, the Egyptian Plover. This species is said to pick food from the teeth of crocodiles, and it certainly takes insects from very near to them, though there are no modern records of a closer relationship.

Coursers and Pratincoles tend to inhabit arid regions, but the Egyptian Plover favours river banks and has the interesting habit of burying its eggs, and even its young, if danger threatens. Much of the incubation of the eggs takes place in the warm sand, and the female probably broods the eggs only at night. It has been recorded that during the day the adult birds will regurgitate water over the eggs in order to cool them. The Egyptian Plover, though clearly a Courser, is aberrant in

ABOVE The Woodcock is a bird of damp woodland floors. The patterned plumage provides excellent camouflage.

OPPOSITE, ABOVE LEFT The Painted Snipe is a bird of fresh-water marshes.

OPPOSITE, ABOVE RIGHT A Water Dikkop photographed at Lake Jipe, Kenya.

OPPOSITE BELOW The Southern (Bush) Stone Curlew stalks its prey.

PAGE 142 The Long-toed Lapwing has a contrasting plumage, which is a feature of the Lapwing group.

144

several ways. The other Coursers are desert birds and, as their name implies, are excellent runners. Rather than fly, the Coursers will sprint from danger and then stand very erect, apparently on tip-toe, to examine the source of the disturbance. Alternatively they will lie flat, neck extended (an attitude which Stone Curlews also adopt), to avoid discovery. The breeding season of Coursers is influenced by the food supply, and, unlike the Egyptian Plover, other Coursers incubate their eggs, though on occasions they merely stand over them to protect them from the heat of the sun.

Pratincoles (Swallow Plovers), in marked contrast to Coursers, are birds of the air, taking their insect food on the wing. They are associated less with arid conditions than Coursers, and are found in open areas like deltas, flood plains, steppe and savanna, where they can hawk for insects over water. Like Stone Curlews they remain active after dark. Unlike most other waders they nest colonially and the young form flocks as soon as they are able to feed themselves. Both Coursers and Pratincoles are notorious vagrants and frequently turn up far outside their normal ranges.

Crab Plovers are not strictly dry-land waders. They follow the tide out, feeding on worms, molluscs and particularly crabs. These they crack with their immensely strong black bills, which are very like those of the bigger Terns. There is only one species of Crab Plover and it has

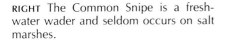

RIGHT The Common Snipe is a fresh-water wader and seldom occurs on salt marshes.

ABOVE Collared Pratincole nesting in picturesque surroundings in south Spain.

LEFT The Red-wattled Lapwing is a typical warm-climate Vanellid.

OPPOSITE A Spotted Thick-knee in the typical dry habitat of the Serengeti, Tanzania.

ABOVE LEFT The Spur-winged Plover is another typical Lapwing.

evolved along its own very separate path. It is a bird of the Indian Ocean, the very hot shorelines of Africa and the Persian Gulf, and its hole-nesting habits combat the extreme heat of these countries. Like most waders it is a sociable species, usually occurring in groups of between five and a hundred, and it is a colonial nester.

Other waders which are birds of the warmer and drier climates are the twenty-five species of Lapwings, three of which occur in South America, eleven in Africa, three in Australasia and four in Oriental habitats; only four are exclusively Palaearctic. Wing-spurs, wattles and crests are features found in the Lapwings which other Plovers lack. They are markedly handsome birds with a variety of contrasting colours and bandings which render them difficult to see when they stand still. It is likely that the group originated in Africa and spread out from there, so Lapwings may be considered to be truly tropical and semi-tropical wader representatives. Whilst Lapwings such as the Sociable Plover may be found occasionally in (post-breeding) flocks of over a thousand birds, it is much more usual to find the different species in small groups of ten to twenty birds outside the breeding season.

The Lapwing of Eurasia is in several ways an exception. It often occurs in large flocks and it is the most northerly breeding member of this family. It is also much more associated with wetlands than are its close relatives and it has recently spread northwards into Iceland and

150

A flock of Senegal Plovers flying over an African plain.

Finland to breed. This is probably connected with the general amelioration in the climate of Europe, where this Lapwing is very common even though its numbers have declined during this century. It is a bird of temperate climates which has evolved from a group of waders which originated in much warmer areas.

The European Woodcock is another aberrant wader of temperate regions which occupies much the same breeding areas across Eurasia. Although it inhabits damp woodlands it does not normally wade and its legs are much shorter than those of other waders. It possesses a long bill, which is sensitive at the tip and is used to probe for earthworms. There can be no doubt that earthworms are an important part of the Woodcock's diet, but it probably takes much more food in the form of insects, millipedes, centipedes, spiders, snails, seeds and berries. Interestingly, Woodcocks are the only waders to have colonized woodlands. Other species may perch and even nest in trees, but they are not woodland birds. Three other Woodcocks are recognized from Asia, and the American Woodcock is a related but much smaller bird. Because of their skulking habits, and the fact that they are often active at dusk, it has been suggested that Woodcocks feed largely at night. Birds fitted with radio transmitters in North America have shown for the most part that they are inactive at night and feed mainly early in the morning, around mid-day and in the evening.

151

152

Woodcocks' eggs tend not to be as pointed as those of most other waders and are paler in ground colour and markings. Amongst leaves they are difficult to see and the bird itself is marvellously camouflaged when incubating.

Woodcocks are the only waders which possess both a long bill and short legs. Usually long bills are found in waders with long legs, but here is an exception, presumably associated with the loss of the wading habit.

At the opposite extreme in bill length are the Seed Snipes, a small group of four species of very aberrant waders which live in South America. As their name implies, they are seed eaters and have a typical seed eater's bill – short, strong and pointed. Their legs are also short, and the birds have the appearance of small Partridges until they take flight. When preparing to fly they usually crouch, and take off at the last moment, when their long, pointed wings, and zigzagging, snipe-like flight, give an indication of their relationships. At a glance they look rather like peculiar Larks or Buntings. They are inhabitants of dry regions, the arid coastlines and stony areas of the high Andes. They possess an interesting adaptation: a flap which covers most of the nostril and prevents the ingress of dust particles from the very dry habitats in which they live. The eggs are wader-like. A clutch of four pear-shaped eggs is laid by each species and all are typically blotched and marked.

However, the eggs of the White-bellied Seed Snipe, which nests on darker coloured soils and heaths, are darker than those of the other three species which nest on paler soils.

The most southerly, and amongst the most aberrant waders, are the Sheathbills, which are Antarctic and sub-Antarctic species. Two species occur and they look rather Pigeon-like, particularly in flight. Whilst on the ground they have the habit of moving about on one leg. In feeding they are true opportunists. During the Penguin breeding season they become virtually parasitic upon them. A Sheathbill will approach a Penguin feeding a chick and harass the pair so much that the parent drops the regurgitated krill. Apart from stealing krill, Sheathbills will also break open unguarded Penguin eggs and attack and kill sickly chicks. During the breeding season of the seals, they will feed on the afterbirth, but at other times of the year Sheathbills will forage on the shoreline. They are the only land birds (birds with unwebbed feet) to penetrate the Antarctic.

The eggs and nest of the Sheathbill are most atypical. The nest may be built in a hole in the rocks, under a boulder, in a crevice or even in an old Petrel hole, and formed from an untidy pile of Penguin feathers, shells, bones and pieces of vegetation. It usually contains two to four grey-white eggs which are blotched brown.

Of the dry-land waders, only the Woodcocks have a long bill, and it is likely that they have evolved from the same stock as the Snipes. Their ancestors were probably wetland birds, and the Woodcocks have reverted at a much later stage to drier habitats. All the other dry-land waders, Stone Curlews, Coursers, Pratincoles, Lapwings and Seed Snipes, have probably evolved from Plover-like stock, birds which were originally of warmer climes. In general, long bills are associated with cold-climate waders and short bills with waders from warmer climates, although there are a few obvious exceptions. For the most part, however, it is likely that long bills have evolved for cold climates, and if they have it is odd that they should have evolved for probing in habitats where for much of the time the substrate may well be impenetrable to any depth. This supports the earlier suggestion that they did not evolve for probing but for removing food items from the base of deep vegetation. It is unlikely that we will ever know for certain, but it is interesting to speculate about the origins of such a remarkable structure as the bill of a wading bird.

The fresh-water shorebirds, birds of wetlands which do not normally inhabit the tideline, are in many ways as unlike the Plovers and Sandpipers as are the dry-land waders. As we have already seen, the Jacanas (which come into this category) have evolved large toes specifically to avoid wading; instead they can trip across floating vegetation with their weight spread over a large area. Most waders are good

OPPOSITE ABOVE A Crowned Lapwing preening itself.

OPPOSITE BELOW The Blacksmith Plover shading her eggs from the sun.

154

LEFT The Australian Spur-winged Plover has large, yellow face wattles.

RIGHT The Banded Plover is an Oriental representative of the Lapwings.

BELOW American Avocets and Black-necked Stilts feed side-by-side in a brackish lagoon in California.

ABOVE Snowy Sheathbill — even in the Antarctic ringed birds confront the photographer.

OPPOSITE The Black-winged Stilt is a bird of warm climates and occurs on fresh-water and salt marshes.

swimmers, but the Jacanas are experts in this field and are capable of diving and submerging to conceal themselves. Sometimes they will flatten themselves on the surface vegetation and remain motionless to avoid detection. Chicks also submerge themselves and like the adults are loath to enter ground cover to hide.

The Painted Snipes are also birds of fresh water, but unlike the Jacanas they skulk in aquatic plants and they have diverged greatly from the main evolutionary lines of the wading birds. Whilst they are Snipe-like in appearance they are not closely related to true Snipes. The Painted Snipe of the Old World has the normal sex roles reversed and the female has a remarkable display in which she folds her wings forward in front of her bill and fans her tail. In this way she attracts a series of males, for each of which she produces a clutch of eggs, and then apparently leaves them to it for the rest of the breeding season.

True Snipes are also birds of fresh water at all times of the year and they are secretive in their habits. They usually feed on marshy ground, where they are not easily seen and they do not take flight until almost trodden on. When flushed they zigzag away, though both the Great Snipe and the Jack Snipe tend to pitch again after flying only a short distance. In the marshy habitat Snipes usually feed by probing deeply, and in this they are one of the few waders which consistently feed in this way. Snipes prefer to forage in almost liquid mud and they often

158

swallow food items without withdrawing the bill. Associated with the deep probing habit is the setting of the eyes far back on the head, and this also occurs in the Woodcocks. In fact Snipes can literally see behind themselves, and they have binocular vision backwards, which enables them to see potential predators whilst feeding. Clearly this is of great advantage and there can be little doubt that the positioning of the eyes has evolved with the probing habit. If other waders' long bills are primarily designed for probing, why then have these waders not evolved backward vision? Could it not be that their long bills have evolved for another purpose altogether and that possibly rear vision has evolved secondarily with probing in Snipes and Woodcocks?

Most species of Snipes are not seen on the shore nor are they as gregarious as many other species of waders. Wisps of five to ten birds are common, and very occasionally up to two thousand can be seen over suitable feeding areas, but this is rare.

There is some argument about how many species of Snipes there are, and some authorities group the American (Wilson's) Snipe, with the Common Snipe, Pina Snipe and African Snipe as a single species, so that there are some eighteen or twenty-one species according to taxonomic taste, if the three Dowitchers are included with them. If Wilson's Snipe and the Common Snipe are regarded as the same species, then the only continents in which it does not occur are Australasia and Antarctica. It is

OPPOSITE White-bellied (left) and Grey-breasted Seed Snipe, anomalous waders of the South American pampas.

BELOW Least Seed Snipe, a Patagonian bird reminiscent of a Sand Grouse.

certainly one of the best-known, if not *the* best-known wader, and Snipe behaviour has become part of the weather-forecasting lore in some areas. Before periods of rain Snipes tend to display at low levels and when high pressure areas approach they perform much higher in the air.

In contrast with the Snipes, Stilts and Avocets are conspicuous birds. Their black and white plumage stands out in the open habitats in which they feed. Stilts tend to be birds of inland lakes and Avocets of shallow, brackish lagoons, though in parts of their ranges both groups occur in fresh-water and marine habitats. Both Stilts and Avocets breed in loose colonies and are found in most parts of the world. The four species of Avocets occur in Australasia, North America, South America and Eurasia and some parts of Africa, whereas of the two species of Stilts, one is confined to Australasia (Banded Stilt) and the other (Black-winged Stilt) is cosmopolitan. Like the Oystercatchers, the Black-winged Stilt occurs in several colour forms in different parts of its range, and in New Zealand one form is completely black.

Whilst most of the waders considered in this chapter vary significantly in one way or another from the Plovers and Sandpipers, perhaps the most aberrant of all is the Ibis-bill which is found in the high plateaux of central Asia and winters as far south as the foothills of the Himalayas. In the past it has been classified with the Stilts and Avocets, but there

The Egyptian Plover often feeds close to crocodiles and consequently is known as the Crocodile Bird.

ABOVE The American Jacana strides out showing its immense feet which are used to spread its weight whilst walking on floating vegetation.

RIGHT The Avocet is a demonstrative bird and behaves aggressively both to its own and other species.

The Ibis-bill is a bird of fast-running mountain streams in Central Asia. It uses its curved bill to collect food items from under stones.

appears to be no particularly good reason for this. It has probably arisen from the same stock as the Plovers, but during its evolution it has diverged significantly from this group. Its bill is decurved like that of an Ibis, but it is a much more slender structure, and it is used for probing below stones of lakes and mountain streams, to extract crustaceans and molluscs. The Ibis-bill usually feeds with the head submerged and its long legs enable it to wade deeply, often up to the belly.

There are, then, waders which seldom wade and others which are not shorebirds, though these are their collective names on each side of the Atlantic. Their variety is an indication of their success as a group and unlike most birds they excel at all three methods of locomotion, being swift runners, fast fliers and, in most cases, good swimmers, though many species avoid swimming. There are some niches into which waders have not diverged: there are no specifically fish-eating or carnivorous waders, nor are there plant eaters or pollen and nectar feeders. Only the small group of Seed Snipes specialize in seeds. However, on the whole, waders have spread into most habitats and niches, and this is particularly the case during the breeding season. In winter many species occupy the same habitat, and for this and other reasons already discussed, it is likely that many of their characteristics were evolved on the breeding grounds. The Knot is one of the commonest waders, but few have seen its nest. There is still much to learn about wading birds, particularly in their nesting areas. Most of what we know already is due to the efforts of amateur ornithologists and almost anyone can still add to the fund of knowledge of this fascinating group of birds.

A Gallery
of Waders

ABOVE A Greenshank removes the shell of a hatched egg from the nest.

LEFT The Caspian Plover is a bird of central Asia.

RIGHT A Purple Sandpiper photographed on its breeding ground in Spitsbergen.

PAGE 166 Dunlins, Sanderlings and Turnstones in the spray at high tide.

PAGE 167 Lapwing alighting on marshy ground in Norfolk.

PAGES 172–3 Oystercatchers at the roost on Hilbre Island.

OPPOSITE Common Sandpiper at the nest with newly hatched chicks.

RIGHT A pair of Water Dikkops wading at Lake Jipe, Kenya.

BELOW A hen Red-necked Phalarope feeding by the edge of a Shetland pond.

ABOVE Little Ringed Plover about to settle on its eggs in typical gravel-pit nesting site.

RIGHT Blackheaded Plover, photographed near the entrance of Tsavo National Park, Kenya.

OPPOSITE Redshanks, Turnstones, Dunlins and Knots roost while waiting for the tide to turn and expose their feeding ground.

ABOVE A Whimbrel approaches her nest in the Shetlands.

OPPOSITE A Black-tailed Godwit at its nest in a Dutch field.

Waders in Camera

The cameras used years ago for wader photography were the Sanderson Field and the Brand 17. The latter was a lightweight, all-metal camera produced in the United States. It had almost the same range of movements as the Sanderson but could also be operated in the hand. Both these cameras were quarter-plate ($4\frac{1}{4}''$ x $3\frac{1}{4}''$ or 10.8 x 8.4cm) in size, and had either glass plates or film packs.

When, in 1934, Ilford Ltd introduced their Soft Gradation Pan plates I used them most of the time but then in 1936 Kodak produced the P800 so I switched to them until, in 1946, they brought out the faster P1200 which were ideal. However, film packs were often far quicker and easier to handle, though much more expensive, and saved reloading the plate holders. My favourites were the Kodak Super XX, Tri-X, and Verichrome Pan and these were exposed according to the prevailing weather conditions.

Just after the war I acquired Sheet Kodachrome in quarter-plate size but it had to be returned to the United States for processing which meant a lengthy wait for the results. When Sheet Ektachrome became available I used this for a time but as the colour balance changed rather a lot from batch to batch I began to use 35mm more frequently. The best emulsions were Kodachrome 2, later replaced by K25, K64 and Ektachrome 200 and 400.

Almost all the photographs were taken in a free and wild state but where I had to resort to an aviary bird this has been made clear in the photographic details.

The old Contax camera, which I worked with immediately after the war, was fitted with a range-finder which worked with lenses up to 135mm but for longer focal lengths a reflex housing was used. When the Contarex appeared in 1963 I adopted this through-the-lens reflex with its range of superb lenses.

In 1970 I obtained the Hasselblad system giving $2\frac{1}{4}''$ x $2\frac{1}{4}''$ (6 x 6cm) because many publishers seemed to prefer the larger format. With this camera I had the 120mm, 150mm, 250mm Zeiss Sonnar, and the 350mm and 500mm Tele-Tessar lenses.

Because Kodachrome was not made larger than 35mm I used the improved Ektachrome film of various speeds, especially E64. But now the Hasselblad outfit is too heavy for me to carry round the world and because 35mm film stock has become so excellent, I have returned to the smaller size.

When the Contarex equipment ceased to be produced in 1973 it was replaced by the Japanese Olympus camera and Zuiko lenses. Their latest model is the OM-2n – surely the wildlife photographer's ideal camera. It has an automatic shutter so all you have to do is set the aperture and the camera automatically uses the right shutter speed. It is amazingly accurate in most circumstances. There is an over-ride which allows you to increase or decrease the automatic exposure when the need arises. I have a range of lenses but those most suited to wader photography are the 135mm, 180mm, 300mm and 600mm. In the few cases where flash has been necessary the Olympus T32 has been advantageous because of the automatic shutter control in the flash out-put.

We use colour transparencies for all our work; if black and white prints are required they are made from the transparencies by first making a negative.

Although we have compiled the following photographic information carefully, full records have not always been kept and in these cases we have given the details believed to be accurate.

Key to Abbreviations

Auto	Automatic Shutter Speed		
HSE	High Speed Ektachrome	K25	Kodachrome 25
EX	Ektachrome X	K64	Kodachrome 64
E64	Ektachrome 64	HSF	High Speed Flash, 1/5000th flash
E200	Ektachrome 200		duration
K2	Kodachrome 2	SFC	Sanderson Field Camera
KX	Kodachrome X	SGP	Ilford Soft Gradation Pan

Endpapers *Wrybills* – Olympus OM-2n, 600mm Zuiko, f/6.5, Auto, K64, New Zealand, 1981.

2–3 *Blacksmith Plovers* – Hasselblad, 500mm Tele-Tessar, f/8, 1/250th, E64, Zimbabwe, 1972.

6 *Curlew* – Olympus OM-2n, 400mm Zuiko, f/6.3, Auto, K64, Hilbre, Cheshire, 1978.

12 *Oystercatchers, Redshanks and Sanderlings* – Hasselblad, 250mm Sonnar, f/8, 1/500th, E200, Hilbre, Cheshire, 1975.

14 *Western Sandpipers* – Olympus OM-2n, 600mm Zuiko, f/8, Auto, K64, California, 1981.

15 *Knots* – Contax, 135mm Sonnar, f/4, 1/500th, Tri-X, Hilbre, Cheshire, 1949.

15 *Grey Plover* – Niall Rankin photograph – no details known.

16 *Killdeer Plover* – Olympus OM-2n, 600mm Zuiko, f/6.5, Auto, K64, California, 1981.

17 *Spur-winged Plover* – Contarex, 250mm Sonnar, f/16, 1/60th, Pan-X, Jordan, 1965.

17 *Turnstones* – Olympus OM-2n, 600mm Zuiko, f/6.5, Auto, K64, Hilbre, Cheshire, 1979.

18 *African Jacana* – Hasselblad, 500mm Tele-Tessar, f/8, 1/250th, E64, Kenya, East Africa, 1977.

19 *Stone Curlew* – Contarex, 250mm Sonnar, f/5.6, 1/250th, Pan-X, Jordan, 1963.

20 *Greenshank* – Hasselblad, 350mm Tele-Tessar, f/5.6, 1/250th, E200, Scotland, 1976.

21 *Banded Stilts* – Olympus OM-2n, 600mm Zuiko, f/6.5, Auto, K64, New Zealand, 1981.

22 *Two-banded Courser* – Olympus OM-2n, 600mm Zuiko, f/6.5, Auto, K64, Kenya, East Africa, 1979.

22 *Snowy Sheathbill* – Olympus OM-2n, 180mm Zuiko, f/5.6, Auto, K64, Antarctic, 1981.

23 *Collared Pratincole* – SFC, 21cm Tessar, f/16, 1/50th, Verichrome film pack, Spain, 1956.

23 *Red-necked Phalarope* – Brand 17, 21cm Tessar, f/16, 1/50th, Super XX, Finland, 1958.

24 *Black-tailed Godwit* – Hasselblad, 500mm Tele-Tessar, f/8, 1/125th, EX, Minsmere, Suffolk, 1975.

25 *Oystercatcher* – SFC, 21cm Tessar, f/11, 1/30th, Sheet Kodachrome, Scotland, 1947.

27 *Redshanks* – Olympus OM-2n, 600mm Zuiko, f/6.5, Auto, K64, Hilbre, Cheshire, 1979.

27 *Spotted Redshank* – Contarex, 400mm Tele-Tessar, f/5.6, 1/125th, EX, Minsmere, Suffolk, 1964.

28 *Golden Plover* – SFC, 21cm Tessar, f/16, 1/30th, P1200, Inverness-shire, 1939.

28 *Little Ringed Plover* – Brand 17, 21cm Tessar, f/16, 1/125th, Super XX, Essex, 1951.

29 *Crab Plover* – Hasselblad, 500mm Tele-Tessar, f/8, 1/500th, HSE, Meda Creek, Kenya, East Africa, 1974.

29 *Bar-tailed Godwit* – Olympus OM-2, 600mm Zuiko, f/6.5, Auto, K64, Hilbre, Cheshire, 1977.

30 *Black Stilt* – Olympus OM-2n, 300mm Zuiko, f/5.6, Auto, K64, Mount Bruce Reserve, New Zealand, 1981.

32 *Turnstone* – Brand 17, 21cm Tessar, f/16, 1/125th, Super XX, Finland, 1958.

32 *Black Turnstone* – Olympus OM-2n, 600mm Zuiko, f/6.5, Auto, K64,

California, 1981.

33 *Long-billed Dowitcher* – Olympus OM-2n, 600mm Zuiko, f/6.5, Auto, K64, California, 1981.

34 *Sanderlings* – Contarex, 250mm Sonnar, f/11, 1/125th, KX, Hilbre, Cheshire, 1962.

35 *Crowned Lapwing* – Olympus OM-2, 600mm Zuiko, f/6.5, Auto, K64, Kenya, East Africa, 1977.

36 *Greater Yellowlegs* – Olympus OM-2n, 600mm Zuiko, f/6.5, Auto, K64, California, 1981.

36 *Ringed Plover* – Hasselblad, 500mm Tele-Tessar, f/8, 1/60th, HSE, Minsmere, Suffolk, 1972.

37 *Ruff* – Contax, 300mm Kilfitt, f/12.5, 1/125th, Tri-X, Minsmere, Suffolk, 1960.

38 *Redshank* – Hasselblad, 250mm Sonnar, f/11, 1/125th, EX, Spain, 1972.

39 *Knots* – SFC, 21cm Tessar, f/22, 1/10th, P1200, Hilbre, Cheshire, 1948.

41 *Lapwing* – SFC, 21cm Tessar, f/11, 1/125th, P800, Norfolk, 1942.

41 *Dunlin* – Contarex, 400mm Tele-Tessar, f/8, 1/250th, EX, Minsmere, Suffolk, 1969.

42 *Golden Plover* – SFC, 21cm Tessar, f/16, 1/30th, P800, Orkney, 1946.

43 *New Zealand Black Oystercatcher* – Olympus OM-2n, 600mm Zuiko, f/6.5, Auto, K64, New Zealand, 1981.

43 *American Black Oystercatcher* – Olympus OM-2n, 600mm Zuiko, f/6.5, Auto, K64, New Zealand, 1981.

44–5 *Black-necked Stilt* – Olympus OM-2n, 600mm Zuiko, f/6.5, Auto, K64, California, 1981.

46 *Ruff* – Contarex, 600mm Kilfitt, f/8, 1/250th, Plus-X, Minsmere, Suffolk, 1968.

46 *Wrybill* – Olympus OM-2n, 600mm Zuiko, f/6.5, Auto, K64, New Zealand, 1981.

47 *Curlew* – SFC, 21cm Tessar, f/11, 1/30th, P800, Yorkshire, 1944.

48 *Golden Plover* – Contarex, 250mm Sonnar, f/11, 1/60th, K2, Norway, 1964.

50 *Dunlins and Ringed Plovers* – Contax, 300mm Kilfitt, f/8, 1/125th, Pan-X, Hilbre, Cheshire, 1948.

50 *Ringed Plover* – Contarex, 600mm Kilfitt, f/8, 1/125th, Pan-X, Minsmere, Suffolk, 1968.

50 *Common Snipe* – Contarex, 400mm Tele-Tessar, f/5.6, 1/250th, Pan-X, Minsmere, Suffolk, 1967.

51 *Red-necked Stints* – Olympus OM-2n, 600mm Zuiko, f/6.5, Auto, K64, New Zealand, 1981.

52 *Whimbrel* – Contarex, 250mm Sonnar, f/8, 1/60th, Pan-X, Shetlands, 1968.

52 *Grey Plover* – Contarex, 600mm Kilfitt, f/5.6, 1/125th, Pan-X, Minsmere, Suffolk, 1964.

53 *Lapwing* – Contarex, 600mm Kilfitt, f/8, 1/60th, K2, Minsmere, Suffolk, 1963.

54 *Oystercatcher* (right) – Contarex, 85mm Sonnar, f/5.6, 1/60th, K2, Hilbre, Cheshire, 1974.

54 *Oystercatcher* (left) – Olympus OM-2n, 100mm Zuiko, f/5.6, 1/60th, K64, Hilbre, Cheshire, 1979.

54 *Little Stint* – Contax, 300mm Kilfitt, f/5.6, 1/125th, Pan-X, Minsmere, Suffolk, 1962.

56 *Wood Sandpiper* – Contarex, 600mm Kilfitt, f/6.3, 1/125th, Pan-X, Minsmere, Suffolk, 1968.

56 *Dunlin* – Contarex, 640mm Novaflex, f/8, 1/250th, HSE, Minsmere, Suffolk, 1974.

56 *Spotted Redshank* – Contarex, 600mm Kilfitt, f/5.6, 1/250th, Plus-X, Minsmere, Suffolk, 1966.

57 *Marsh Sandpiper* – Hasselblad, 500mm Tele-Tessar, f/8, 1/250th, EX, Zimbabwe, 1972.

58 *Curlew Sandpiper* – Contarex, 600mm Kilfitt, f/8, 1/60th, EX, Minsmere, Suffolk, 1966.

59 *Surf Birds* – Olympus OM-2n, 600mm Zuiko, f/6.5, Auto, K64, California, 1981.

59 *Pectoral Sandpiper* – Niall Rankin photograph – no details known.

60 *Common Sandpiper* – Contarex, 600mm Kilfitt, f/8, 1/60th, K2, Minsmere, Suffolk, 1964.

60 *Green Sandpiper* – Contarex, 400mm Tele-Tessar, f/5.6, 1/250th, K2, Minsmere, Suffolk, 1964.

61 *Black-tailed Godwits* – Contarex, 600mm Kilfitt, f/6.3, 1/125th, Pan-X, Minsmere, Suffolk, 1966.

62 *Stone Curlew* – Brand 17, 21cm Tessar, f/22, 1/15th, Verichrome, Minsmere, Suffolk, 1950.

63 *Red-necked Phalarope* – Contarex, 600mm Kilfitt, f/5.6, 1/125th, K2, Shetlands, 1968.

63 *Avocet* – Contarex, 1000mm MTO, f/12.5, 1/250th, HSE, Minsmere, Suffolk, 1974.

64 *Water Dikkop* – Hasselblad, 350mm Tele-Tessar, f/5.6, 1/250th, E64, Kenya, East Africa, 1977.

64 *Snowy Sheathbill* – Niall Rankin photograph – no details known.

66 *Black-winged Stilts* – Hasselblad, 500mm Tele-Tessar, f/8, 1/250th, EX, Spain, 1972.

68 *Curlews* – Contarex, 250mm Sonnar, f/5.6, 1/500th, Plus-X, Pakistan, 1965.

69 *Redshank* – Olympus OM-2n, 600mm Zuiko, f/6.5, Auto, K64, Hilbre, Cheshire, 1980.

69 *Dunlin* – Contarex, 600mm Kilfitt, f/5.6, 1/500th, K64, Minsmere, Suffolk, 1974.

70 *Greenshank* – SFC, 21cm Tessar, f/16, 1/50th, SGP, Inverness-shire, 1940.

71 *Wood Sandpipers* – Hasselblad, 500mm Tele-Tessar, f/8, 1/250th, EX, Zimbabwe, 1972.

72 *Common Snipe* – Olympus OM-1, 600mm Zuiko, f/6.5, 1/125th, K64, Minsmere, Suffolk, 1975.

72 *Collared Pratincole* – Brand 17, 21cm Tessar, f/32, 1/30th, P1200, Spain, 1956.

73 *Ringed Plover* (both pictures) – SFC, 21cm Tessar, f/22, 1/30th, P1200, Suffolk, 1948.

74 *Lapwing* – Contarex, 300mm Kilfitt, f/5.6, 1/250th, Pan-X, Minsmere, Suffolk, 1970.

74 *Kittlitz's Plover* – Hasselblad, 500mm Tele-Tessar, f/8, 1/250th, Plus-X, Zimbabwe, 1972.

75 *Avocet* – Hasselblad, 350mm Tele-Tessar, f/5.6, 1/250th, EX, Minsmere, Suffolk, 1973.

76 *Avocet* – Brand 17, 21cm Tessar, f/22, 1/30th, P1200, Holland, 1952.

77 *Ruff* – Contarex, 600mm Kilfitt, f/5.6, 1/125th, EX, Minsmere, Suffolk, 1973.

77 *Dotterel* – Leica, 135mm Leitz, f/5.6, 1/50th, Pan-X, Inverness-shire, 1939.

77 *Ringed Plover* – Contax, 135mm Tessar, f/5.6, 1/50th, Pan-X, Kent, 1945.

78–9 *Avocets* – Hasselblad, 250mm Sonnar, f/16, 1/60th, E64, Spain, 1972.

81 *Ringed Plover* – SFC, 21cm Tessar, f/16, 1/30th, Sheet Kodachrome, Suffolk, 1945.

81 *Ruffs* – Brand 17, 21cm Tessar, f/16, 1/30th, Sheet Ektachrome, Holland, 1952.

82 *Stone Curlew* – SFC, 21cm Tessar, f/11, 1/30th, Sheet Kodachrome, Suffolk, 1945.

83 *Greenshank* – SFC, 21cm Tessar, f/16, 1/30th, P1200, Inverness-shire, 1947.

84 *Common Snipe* – SFC, 21cm Tessar, f/8, 1/50th, Sheet Kodachrome, Suffolk, 1945.

86–9 *Nests and eggs* – no details kept.

90 *Redshank* – SFC, 21cm Tessar, f/16, 1/10th, SGP, Norfolk, 1943.

90 *Kentish Plover* – Brand 17, 21cm Tessar, f/16, 1/30th, Verichrome, Holland, 1952.

91 *Kentish Plover* – Brand 17, 21cm Tessar, f/22, 1/50th, Super XX, Spain, 1956.

92 *Stone Curlew* – SFC, 8½″ Dallmeyer Serrac, f/11, 1/30th, SGP, Suffolk, 1936.

92 *Dotterel* – Contax, 135mm Sonnar, f/5.6, 1/50th, K2, Finland, 1958.

93 *Oystercatcher* – Hasselblad, 140–280mm Schneider zoom, f/8, 1/125th, E64, Suffolk, 1982, David Hosking.

94 *Ringed Plover* – SFC, 21cm Tessar, f/22, 1/20th, Super XX, Suffolk, 1946.

94 *Killdeer Plover* – Niall Rankin photograph – no details known.

95 *Whimbrel* – Contarex, 250mm Sonnar, f/11, 1/60th, K2, Shetlands, 1968.

96 *Grey Plover* – Niall Rankin photograph – no details known.

97 *Black-winged Stilt* – Hasselblad, 250mm Sonnar, f/5.6, 1/250th, EX, Spain, 1972.

98 *Greater Sand Plover* – Contarex, 600mm Kilfitt, f/5.6, 1/250th, Pan-X, Jordan, 1963.

98 *Temminck's Stint* – Brand 17, 21cm Tessar, f/8, 1/50th, Sheet Ektachrome, Finland, 1958.

99 *Greenshank* – Olympus OM-2, 300mm Zuiko, f/11, 1/60th, Pan-X, Scotland, 1976.

100 *Woodcock* – Hasselblad, 250mm Sonnar, f/5.6, 1/250th, EX, Scotland, 1973.

101 *Wood Sandpiper* – Brand 17, 21cm Tessar, f/22, 1/50th, Super XX, Finland, 1958.

102 *Terek Sandpiper* – Brand 17, 21cm Tessar, f/22, 1/50th, Super XX, Finland, 1958.

102 *Reeve* – Contarex, 250mm Sonnar, f/8, 1/250th, K2, Norway, 1964.

103 *Western Sandpiper* – Niall Rankin photograph – no details known.

103 *Purple Sandpiper* – Niall Rankin photograph – no details known.

104 *Common Sandpiper* – SFC, 21cm Tessar, f/16, 1/20th, P800, Wales, 1937.

104 *Grey Phalarope* – Niall Rankin photograph – no details known.

104 *Ruff* – Contax, 50mm Tessar, f/8, 1/125th, Pan-X, Norway, 1964.

105 *Curlew* – Contarex, 50mm Plannar, f/5.6, 1/125th, K2, Shetlands, 1968.

105 *Whimbrel* – Contarex, 50mm Plannar, f/5.6, 1/125th, K2, Shetlands, 1968.

106 *Stone Curlew* – Contax, 50mm Tessar, f/11, 1/50th, Pan-X, Suffolk, 1945.

106 *Avocet* – Brand 17, 21cm Tessar, f/11, 1/125th, Verichrome, Suffolk, 1950.

108 *Curlew Sandpiper* – Hasselblad, 500mm Tele-Tessar, f/8, 1/500th, HSE, Kenya, East Africa, 1974.

110 *Sanderlings* – Olympus OM-2n, 600mm Zuiko, f/6.5, Auto, K64, California, 1981.

110 *Knot* – Contarex, 600mm Kilfitt, f/5.6, 1/250th, K2, Minsmere, Suffolk, 1970.

111 *Sanderlings and Dunlins* – Contarex, 250mm Sonnar, f/5.6, 1/500th, Pan-X, Hilbre, Cheshire, 1968.

112 *Spotted Redshank* – Contarex, 600mm Kilfitt, f/5.6, 1/60th, Pan-X, Minsmere, Suffolk, 1969.

113 *Long-billed Curlew* – Olympus OM-2n, 600mm Zuiko, f/6.5, Auto, K64, California, 1981.

113 *Marbled Godwit* – Olympus OM-2n, 600mm Zuiko, f/6.5, Auto, K64, California, 1981.

114 *Greater Yellowlegs* – Olympus OM-2n, 600mm Zuiko, f/6.5, Auto, K64, California, 1981.

115 *Lapwings* – Hasselblad, 500mm Tele-Tessar, f/8, 1/500th, E200, Gloucestershire, 1975.

116–17 *Sanderlings* – Contarex, 250mm Sonnar, f/5.6, 1/500th, KX, Hilbre, Cheshire, 1965.

118 *Oystercatchers etc.* – Contarex, 600mm Kilfitt, f/5.6, 1/1000th, Plus-X, Hilbre, Cheshire, 1970.

119 *Least Sandpiper* – Olympus OM-2n, 600mm Zuiko, f/6.5, Auto, K64, California, 1981.

119 *Solitary Sandpiper* – Olympus OM-1, 400mm Zuiko, f/8, 1/250th, K64, Amazon, 1975, David Hosking.

120 *Willet* – Olympus OM-2n, 600mm Zuiko, f/6.5, Auto, K64, California, 1981.

121 *Redshanks* – Brand 17, 21cm Tessar, f/16, 1/30th, P1200, Hilbre, Cheshire, 1950.

122 *Redshanks and Turnstones* – Olympus OM-2n, 600mm Zuiko, f/6.5, Auto, Pan-X, Hilbre, Cheshire, 1979.

123 *Sharp-tailed Sandpiper* – Olympus OM-2n, 600mm Zuiko, f/6.5, Auto, K64, Australia, 1981.

123 *Lapwing* – Contarex, 600mm Kilfitt, f/5.6, 1/125th, Pan-X, Minsmere, Suffolk, 1968.

124 *Knots, Oystercatchers and Herring Gulls* – Brand 17, 21cm Tessar, f/32, 1/15th, P1200, Hilbre, Cheshire, 1948.

124 *Knots* – Olympus OM-2n, 600mm Zuiko, f/6.5, Auto, K64, New Zealand, 1981.

126 *Knots, Dunlins, Turnstones, Redshanks and Sanderlings* – Hasselblad, 350mm Tele-Tessar, f/8, 1/250th, E64, Hilbre, Cheshire, 1977.

129 *Knots, Dunlins, Redshanks and Curlews* – Contarex, 600mm Kilfitt, f/5.6, 1/500th, Tri-X, Hilbre, Cheshire, 1971.

129 *Oystercatchers and Curlews* – SFC, 21cm Tessar, f/16, 1/250th, Super XX, Hilbre, Cheshire, 1946.

130 *Redshanks* – Olympus OM-2n, 600mm Zuiko, f/6.5, Auto, K64, Hilbre, Cheshire, 1978.

131 *Redshanks* – Olympus OM-2, 400mm Zuiko, f/6.3, Auto, E200, Hilbre, Cheshire, 1976.

132–3 *Dunlins* – Brand 17, 21cm Tessar, f/32, 1/10th, Sheet Kodachrome, Hilbre, Cheshire, 1948.

134 *Knots* – Brand 17, 21cm Tessar, f/22, 1/30th, Super XX, Hilbre, Cheshire, 1949.

134 *Kentish Plover* – Olympus OM-2n, 600mm Zuiko, f/6.5, Auto, K64, California, 1981.

135 *Grey Plover* – Olympus OM-2n, 600mm Zuiko, f/6.5, Auto, K64, Hilbre, Cheshire, 1980.

136 *Turnstones and Knots* – SFC, 21cm Tessar, f/22, 1/30th, Sheet Kodachrome, Hilbre, Cheshire, 1947.

138 *Sanderlings* – Contarex, 250mm Sonnar, f/5.6, 1/500th, Pan-X, Hilbre, Cheshire, 1967.

139 *Aerial view* – Olympus OM-2n, 85mm Zuiko, f/8, Auto, K64, Ribble, Lancashire, 1982, David Hosking.

139 *Knots etc.* – Hasselblad, 250mm Sonnar, f/8, 1/125th, EX, Hilbre, Cheshire, 1977.

140 *Willet and Whimbrel* – Olympus OM-2n, 600mm Zuiko, f/6.5, Auto, K64, California, 1981.

140 *Mixed flock of waders* – Contarex, 250mm Sonnar, f/5.6, 1/500th, Pan-X, Hilbre, Cheshire, 1967.

141 *Aerial roost* – Contarex, 250mm Sonnar, f/5.6, 1/1000th, Tri-X, Hilbre, Cheshire, 1968.

142 *Long-toed Lapwing* – Olympus OM-2, 600mm Zuiko, f/6.5, Auto, K64, Kenya, East Africa, 1977.

144 *Woodcock* – SFC, 21cm Tessar, f/8, Sashalite flashbulb, Super XX, Wales,

List of Scientific and English Names

This list has been modified from that appearing in J. L. Peters' *Checklist of Birds of the World*, Vol. 2, Harvard University Press, Cambridge, USA (1934), to take account of more recent studies, particularly those of Sibley (1960) and Jehl (1968), and it is limited to specific names. No attempt has been made to list the sub-species which have been named in the past as these are too numerous and many cannot be justified as they are from populations which form part of a continuous gradation or cline.

Argument still exists about the validity of some species, particularly the Oystercatchers, and this list differs from others recently published because of this. For example, some authorities consider the Common Snipe to be the same species on each side of the Atlantic; others regard it as two species.

This list has the various groups arranged in order of likely relationship but future work will, no doubt, require modifications to the order given here. In addition some species given specific status here may be found to be conspecific with others so that the overall numbers of wader species might, in fact, be two or three fewer than is listed here.

SUBORDER: CHARADRII

SUPERFAMILY: *JACANOIDEA*

FAMILY: *JACANIDAE*
(Jacanas)
Smaller Jacana	*Microparra capensis*
African Jacana	*Actophilornis africana*
Madagascar Jacana	*A. albinucha*
Comb-crested Jacana	*Irediparra gallinacea*
Pheasant-tailed Jacana	*Hydrophasianus chirurgus*
Bronze-winged Jacana	*Metopidius indicus*
American Jacana	*Jacana spinosa*

FAMILY: *ROSTRATULIDAE*
(Painted Snipes)
Painted Snipe	*Rostratula benghalensis*
South American Painted Snipe	*Nycticryphes semi-collaris*

SUPERFAMILY: *CHARADRIOIDEA*

FAMILY: *HAEMATOPODIDAE*
(Oystercatchers)
Oystercatcher	*Haematopus ostralegus*
Black Oystercatcher	*H. bachmani*
American Oystercatcher	*H. palliatus*
Magellanic Oystercatcher	*H. leucopodus*
Sooty Oystercatcher	*H. fuliginosus*
Blackish Oystercatcher	*H. ater*

FAMILY: *RECURVIROSTRIDAE*
(Avocets and Stilts)
Black-winged Stilt	*Himantopus himantopus*
Banded Stilt	*Cladorhynchus leucocephala*
Avocet	*Recurvirostra avosetta*
American Avocet	*R. americana*
Red-necked Avocet	*R. novae-hollandiae*
Andean Avocet	*R. andina*

FAMILY: *BURHINIDAE*
(Stone Curlews)
Stone Curlew	*Burhinus oedicnemus*
Senegal Thick-knee	*B. senegalensis*
Water Thick-knee	*B. vermiculatus*
Spotted Thick-knee	*B. capensis*
Double-striped Thick-knee	*B. bistriatus*
Peruvian Thick-knee	*B. superciliaris*
Southern Stone Curlew	*B. magnirostris*
Great Stone Curlew	*Esacus recurvirostris*
Beach Stone Curlew	*Orthorhamphus magnirostris*

FAMILY: *CHARADRIIDAE*
(Plovers)

SUBFAMILY: *VANELLINAE*
White-tailed Plover	*Chettusia leucura*
Sociable Plover	*C. gregaria*
Lapwing	*Vanellus vanellus*
Southern Lapwing	*Belonopterus chilensis*
Long-toed Lapwing	*Hemiparra crassirostris*
Spot-breasted Plover	*Tylibyx melanocephalus*
Grey-headed Lapwing	*Microsarcops cinereus*
Red-wattled Lapwing	*Lobivanellus indicus*
White-crowned Plover	*Ziphidiopterus albiceps*
Javanese Lapwing	*Rogibyx tricolor*
Australian Spur-winged Plover	*Lobibyx novae-hollandiae*
Masked Plover	*L. miles*
Wattled Plover	*Afribyx senegallus*
Senegal Plover	*Stephanibyx lugubris*
Black-winged Plover	*S. melanopterus*
Crowned Lapwing	*S. coronatus*
Spur-winged Lapwing	*Hoplopterus spinosus*
Blacksmith Plover	*H. armatus*
Indian Spur-winged Lapwing	*H. duvaucelii*
Pied Plover	*Hoploxypterus cayanus*
Andean Lapwing	*Ptiloscelys resplendens*
Banded Plover	*Zonifer tricolor*
Brown-chested Plover	*Anomalophrys superciliosus*
Yellow-wattled Lapwing	*Lopipluvia malarbarica*
Blackheaded Plover	*Sarciophorus tectus*

SUBFAMILY: *CHARADRIINAE*
Grey Plover	*Squatarola squatarola*
Golden Plover	*Pluvialis apricaria*
Lesser Golden Plover	*P. dominica*
Red-breasted Dotterel	*Pluviorhynchus obscurus*
Hooded Dotterel	*Charadrius rubricollis*
Ringed Plover	*C. hiaticula*
Semi-palmated Plover	*C. semipalmatus*
Piping Plover	*C. melodus*
Little Ringed Plover	*C. dubius*
Kentish Plover	*C. alexandrinus*
Chestnut-banded Plover	*C. venustus*
Two-banded Plover	*C. falklandicus*
Puna Plover	*C. alticola*
Banded Dotterel	*C. bicinctus*
Malay Plover	*C. peronii*
Collared Plover	*C. collaris*
Kittlitz's Plover	*C. pecuarius*
Wire Bird	*C. sanctae-helenae*
Black-banded Sand Plover	*C. thoracicus*
Long-billed Ringed Plover	*C. placidus*
Killdeer Plover	*C. vociferus*
Three-banded Plover	*C. tricollaris*
Mongolian Plover	*C. mongolus*
Wilson's Plover	*C. wilsonia*
Greater Sand Plover	*C. leschenaultii*
Black-fronted Plover	*Elseyornis melanops*
Caspian Plover	*Eupoda asiatica*
Oriental Plover	*E. veredus*
Mountain Plover	*E. montana*
Tawny-throated Dotterel	*Oreophilus ruficollis*
Red-kneed Dotterel	*Erythrogonys cinctus*
Dotterel	*Eudromias morinellus*

182

Rufous-chested Dotterel	Zonibyx modestus
New Zealand Shore Plover	Thinornis novae-seelandiae
Australian Dotterel	Peltohyas australis
Wrybill	Anarhynchus frontalis
Magellanic Plover	Pluvianellus socialis

SUBFAMILY: *PHEGORNITHINAE*

Diademed Sandpiper-Plover	Phegornis mitchellii

FAMILY: *GLAREOLIDAE*
(Coursers and Pratincoles)

SUBFAMILY: *CURSORIINAE*

Egyptian Plover	Pluvianus aegyptius
Cream-coloured Courser	Cursorius cursor
Temminck's Courser	C. temminckii
Indian Courser	C. coromandelicus
Two-banded Courser	Rhinoptilus africanus
Heuglin's Courser	R. cinctus
Violet-tipped Courser	R. chalcopterus
Jerdon's Courser	R. bitorquatus

SUBFAMILY: *GLAREOLINAE*

Long-legged Pratincole	Stiltia isabella
Collared Pratincole	Glareola pratincola
Eastern Collared Pratincole	G. maldivarum
Black-winged Pratincole	G. nordmanni
Madagascar Pratincole	G. ocularis
White-collared Pratincole	G. nuchalis
Grey Pratincole	G. cinerea
Little Pratincole	G. lactea

FAMILY: *SCOLOPACIDAE*
(Sandpipers and Snipes)

SUBFAMILY: *TRINGINAE*

TRIBE: *NUMENINI*

Upland (Bartram's) Sandpiper	Bartramia longicauda
Little Curlew	Numenius minutus
Eskimo Curlew	N. borealis
Whimbrel	N. phaeopus
Bristle-thighed Curlew	N. tahitiensis
Slender-billed Curlew	N. tenuirostris
Eurasian Curlew	N. arquata
Far Eastern Curlew	N. madagascariensis
Long-billed Curlew	N. americanus
Black-tailed Godwit	Limosa limosa
Hudsonian Godwit	L. haemastica
Bar-tailed Godwit	L. lapponica
Marbled Godwit	L. fedoa

TRIBE: *TRINGINI*

Spotted Redshank	Tringa erythropus
Redshank	T. totanus
Lesser Yellowlegs	T. flavipes
Marsh Sandpiper	T. stagnatalis
Greenshank	T. nebularia
Greater Yellowlegs	T. melanoleuca
Green Sandpiper	T. ocrophus
Solitary Sandpiper	T. solitaria
Wood Sandpiper	T. glareola
Spotted Greenshank	T. guttifer
Terek Sandpiper	T. cinerea
Common Sandpiper	T. hypoleucos
Spotted Sandpiper	T. macularia
Willet	Catoptrophorus semipalmatus
Grey-rumped Sandpiper	Heteroscelus brevipes
Wandering Tattler	H. incanus

TRIBE: *PROSOBONINI*

Tuamatu Sandpiper	Aechmorhynchus parvirostris

SUBFAMILY: *ARENARIINAE*

Turnstone	Arenaria interpres
Black Turnstone	A. melanocephala

SUBFAMILY: *PHALAROPODINAE*

Grey Phalarope	Phalaropus fulicarius
Wilson's Phalarope	Steganops tricolor
Red-necked Phalarope	Lobipes lobatus

SUBFAMILY: *SCOLOPACINAE*

Eurasian Woodcock	Scolopax rusticola
East Indian Woodcock	S. saturata
Celebes Woodcock	S. celebensis
Obi Woodcock	S. rochussenii
American Woodcock	Philohela minor

SUBFAMILY: *CAPELLINAE*

Short-billed Dowitcher	Limnodromus griseus
Long-billed Dowitcher	L. scolopaceus
Asian Dowitcher	L. semipalmatus
Sub-Antarctic Snipe	Coenocorypha aucklandica
Solitary Snipe	Capella solitaria
Japanese Snipe	C. hardwickii
Wood Snipe	C, nemoricola
Pintail Snipe	C. stenura
Swinhoe's Snipe	C. megala
African Snipe	C. nigripennis
Madagascar Snipe	C. macrodactyla
Great Snipe	C. media
Common Snipe	C. gallinago
Noble Snipe	C. nobilis
Giant Snipe	C. undulata
Banded Snipe	Chubbia imperialis
Jameson's Snipe	C. jamesoni
Cordilleran Snipe	C. stricklandii
Jack Snipe	Lymnocryptes minima

SUBFAMILY: *CALIDRIINAE*

Knot	Calidris canutus
Great Knot	C. tenuirostris
Sanderling	C. alba
Semi-palmated Sandpiper	C. pusillus
Western Sandpiper	C. mauri
Spoon-billed Sandpiper	C. pygmeus
Red-necked Stint	C. ruficollis
Little Stint	C. minuta
Temminck's Stint	C. temminckii
Long-toed Stint	C. subminuta
Least Sandpiper	C. minutilla
White-rumped Sandpiper	C. fuscicollis
Baird's Sandpiper	C. bairdii
Pectoral Sandpiper	C. melanotus
Sharp-tailed Sandpiper	C. acuminata
Purple Sandpiper	C. maritima
Rock Sandpiper	C. ptilocnemis
Dunlin	C. alpina
Curlew Sandpiper	C. testacea
Broad-billed Sandpiper	Limicola falcinellus
Stilt Sandpiper	Micropalama himantopus
Buff-breasted Sandpiper	Tryngites subruficollis
Ruff	Philomachus pugnax

SUBFAMILY: *APHRIZINAE*

Surf Bird	Aphriza virgata

SUPERFAMILY: *IBIDORHYNCHOIDEA*

FAMILY: *IBIDORHYNCHIDAE*
(Ibis-bills)

Ibis-bill	Ibidorhyncha struthersii

SUPERFAMILY: *DROMADOIDEA*

FAMILY: *DROMADIDAE*
(Crab Plovers)

Crab Plover	Dromas ardeola

SUPERFAMILY: *CHIONIDOIDEA*

FAMILY: *THINOCORIDAE*
(Seed Snipes)

Rufous-bellied Seed Snipe	Attagis gayi
White-bellied Seed Snipe	A. malouinus
Grey-breasted Seed Snipe	Thinocorus orbignyianus
Least Seed Snipe	T. rumicivorus

FAMILY: *CHIONIDIDAE*
(Sheathbills)

Snowy Sheathbill	Chionis alba
Black-faced Sheathbill	C. minor

Index

Page numbers in *italic* refer to the illustrations